M

CW00644752

Modern Music Masters Manic Street Preachers

Stephen Lee Naish

DEDICATION

The Modern Music Masters series of books is the brainchild of Tom Boniface-Webb, my huge thanks to him for the commission and support of this book.

I would also like to thank the many fans of Manic Street Preachers who I have connected with over the past few years. Being immersed in the world of the Manics has been made more exciting by being able to share and respond together.
Thank you for liking and retweeting my Manics based 'dad-jokes'.

As always, thanks to Jamie, Hayden and Isla.

CONTENTS

Acknowledgments   i

n.b. all tracks written by James Dean Bradfield, Nicky Wire (née Jones), and Sean Moore, unless otherwise stipulated

ACKNOWLEDGMENTS

Thank you to all the following, without whom this book would not have been possible:

Cover Design: Barry Parkinson at www.beepea.co.uk
Martin Talbot, Chief Executive, Official Charts Company
Rob Poole, Commercial Manager, Official Charts Company

The Modern Music Masters series is now published in partnership with the UK Official Charts Company.

Books in the Modern Music Masters Series:

Oasis
Blur
Pulp
Manic Street Preachers
The Verve
Suede
Paul Weller – The Solo Years

Series editor: Tom Boniface-Webb

MMM4 – Manic Street Preachers Spotify Playlist

Available at: MMM4 – Manic Street Preachers

PREFACE:

Welcome to *Modern Music Masters*, a series of books chronicling the stories behind many of the UK's favourite music artists and which are supported by the Official Charts Company.

This volume focuses on one of the most long-lasting and successful Welsh groups of all time, Manic Street Preachers, still going today after more than 30 years together.

The Official Charts have been chronicling the British public's love of music over eight different decades now, from the Fifties right through to the current day. And, in doing so, they have reflected the way that music is consumed and listened to in many different ways, from 78 RPM discs in the Fifties right through to the streaming services of today.

As well as being the ultimate reflection of music fandom, the Official Charts – both singles and albums – are one of the few places where artists can take on their peers every week, and reflect the evolution of their careers, the highs and lows, through their Number 1s, their Top 10s and the chart positions they might rather forget. That is the same today as it has ever been.

We hope you enjoy tracing the journeys of these musical icons, through the Official Charts and beyond.

Martin Talbot
Chief Executive, Official Charts Company
November 2021

FOREWORD:

Manic Street Preachers are one of Britain's biggest indie-rock bands, and one of the few groups that can properly lay a claim to being as versatile and eclectic as rock music will allow a band to be. To think that the band that wrote Motown Junk is the same one that wrote Ocean Spray is to consider the distance that they have travelled since they first formed in the mid-eighties. And what a journey it has been, from the idealistic four young men from South Wales, to the three older, wiser men of the world, that the grown up Manics now are. A mammoth 13 studio albums over 26 years, not to mention the plethora of B-sides, EPs and solo albums that have added to their incredible back catalogue.

Putting the tragedy of Richey Edwards aside – Steve will go into plenty of detail about Richey's sad story – the heart of the Manics, the very essence that has kept them going all of these years, is the friendship that sits in the midst of their story. James Dean Bradfield, Sean Moore and Nicky Wire share not only a background but also an ideology of how the world should and could be, and they are only too happy to share their thoughts in song. They are as interested in the world as rock stars could be, choosing to write songs about class, culture, alienation, boredom, and despair, as well as working-class hymns of pride. In their quarter of a century, they have re-defined what it is to be an intelligent working-class band and they are far from done yet.

Welcome to *Modern Music Masters – Manic Street Preachers*, the fourth in the series, and the first not to be written by me. It has been a pleasure to hand over authorship for the first time to the very talented Stephen Lee Naish, who has written extensively on music and film, and has already published one book on the Manics, the excellent deconstruction of the band's 2001 album, *Know Your Enemy*, 2018's *Riffs and Meaning*.

As always, this book doesn't pretend to be a definitive biography of the band. Sadly, there was lots that had to be left out to make sure that it sticks to the Modern Music Masters' format of 50,000 words. Each book acts as something of an introduction to the band and their music, focusing on the singles and albums they released, and the charts they were released into. If you're looking for a closer study of every move the band made, then this might not be the book for you.

That said, Steve has decided to tell the Manics story his way, and whilst remaining faithful to the overall series, the book is structured slightly differently to the previous editions. The top 10s surrounding the band's releases have been removed because this fits better with the narrative. Instead, there is much more on the Manics' music, and Steve goes into incredibly in-depth detail on even the most remote B-side.

In addition to the books that Steve will mention, the other books on the Manics that I have enjoyed over the years, some still claiming a spot on my bookshelf, you don't need to go much further than *Manic Street Preachers: Sweet Venom* by Martin Clarke (Plexus, 1997); as well as David Evans' excellent analysis of *The Holy Bible* for 33 1/3 (2019); and Nicky Wire's ex-girlfriend's book *In the Beginning: My Life with the Manic Street Preachers* by Jennifer Watkins-Isnardi (John Blake, 2000).

Once again, we hope you enjoy reading this

book about one of British music's most loved bands, as much as we have loved losing ourselves in the music and band's story. Stay tuned for more editions to the MMM series later this year. And don't forget to let us know what you think.

Tom Boniface-Webb
November 2021

A FEW WORDS FROM THE AUTHOR

What is astounding about Manic Street Preachers is their continued ability to engage and surprise their listeners. Thirty-plus years in the game has not dulled the band's instincts to make challenging, uplifting, melancholic, and politically charged music that always manages to contain lyrical rabbit holes to tumble into and explore further. Take, for example, the band's 2018 album *Resistance is Futile*, the most recent, at least at the time of this writing. The first single to be pulled from *Resistance is Futile* was International Blue, a bright and shiny rock standard that rattled along with a danceable bounce reminiscent of Bruce Springsteen's 1980s hit Dancing in The Dark. Alongside its jaunty tune, the lyrical content explored the life and work of French artist Yves Klein. On that same record, one found the song Hold Me Like a Heaven which soured away on a spine-tingling choral backing vocal and, with its title, referenced Phillip Larkin's poem Lines on A Young Lady's Photograph Album. To think that at this point in their career, Manic Street Preachers can still pull songs like International Blue and Hold Me Like a Heaven out of their collective back pockets boggles the mind.

Alongside these two songs are another set of tracks that contained pointers introducing or acquainting listeners to another line-up of icons and events from history. Alongside Klein and Larkin, we have songs on the Welsh poet Dylan Thomas and his stormy marriage to the author Caitlin Thomas, the low-key artistic triumph of American photographer Vivian Maier, an acknowledgment of the divine beauty talent of David Bowie, as well as a tribute to the triumph of the Justice for The Victims of Hillsborough campaign. It is striking that the band still places the intelligence and education of their listeners above all else. A simple quote on a record sleeve is often all it takes to send this author spiralling into the abyss of books, records, and films to fill in the gaps. This is something of a Manic Street Preachers party trick. One that we continue to love them for and one that this text will continuously encounter.

Of course, the natural conclusion to this is that fans of the band have also become well-read and, if not educated through academia, have at the very least educated themselves. And over the past ten years or so, as fans of the band who were swept up in the early to mid-1990s and beyond have aged into academic jobs, journalism, or writing and creative acts of some kind, studies have been written about the band's career and certain records. From Simon Price's outstanding biography *Everything: A Book About Manic Street Preachers* to *Triptych: Three Studies of The Holy Bible*, Matthijs Peters academic text *Popular Music, Critique and Manic Street Preachers* to Rob Jovanovic's *A Version of Reason: In Search of Richey Edwards*. Back in the late 1980s and early 1990s, the band was one of many to be featured heavily in fanzines during heyday and the recent resurgence of fanzines online and in print on the band and even the dedicated podcast *Do You Love Us?* (Now called *What is Music?* as they branch out to other bands) which provides a blow-by-blow account of each of the band's records and the contextual nature of the band's lyrics, have enlivened the Manics among the fans and casual listeners. Fans of Manic Street Preachers are finding new and inventive ways to engage with the music, lyrics, and culture that surrounds them.

The trajectory of all those involved in these creative endeavours, from the podcast to the polemic, is pretty much the same; alone in a teenage bedroom, copies of *NME* and *Melody Maker* discarded on the floor whilst pouring over the lyrics of the band's early records and rereading interviews for recommended books and films to supplement the recordings. It is a cliché, but a truism, nonetheless. I was one of these teenage kid's desperately playing cultural catch-up after discovering the band in the mid-1990s and I went on to write a book on the band. This one, yes, but also another titled *Riffs and Meaning*. That book pondered the exceptional nature of the band's sixth record *Know Your Enemy* (2001). Whilst that study attempted to offer the reader an argument and a cluster of opinions (some popular, some less so), this book is different in that it intends to offer a more linear historical overview of the band's records and singles from predominantly a British perspective and one told through record releases, chart performances and live appearances. This book is meant to offer a brisk and concise skip through the band's career, but as we go, I'll point out other books, documentaries, and other studies to direct the reader further.

The Manics story is one of rise, fall, rise, fall and rise again and the band's success is tied up with the shifts in British and Welsh culture and whilst pockets of fandom exist elsewhere in the world (Japan in particular) the consistency of the band's fortunes is a mainly British concern.

Though the Manics comfortably lived outside of the British rock establishment and the Britpop subgenre, undoubtedly, they benefited greatly from the success of bands like Oasis, Blur, and Pulp in the mid-1990s, though they have long left these bands coughing in the dust of the immense success they have achieved since Britpop crashed and burned in the late 1990s.

We will take the journey album by album and single by single, pausing to reflect on key tracks and live performances. But to better digest the story, we will break the band's history into clusters, or eras, starting with the first chapter 'There is Work to be Done' and their beginnings in the Welsh ex-mining town of Blackwood and the early punk rumblings of their first singles and EPs. Chapter Two, 'Scream to a Sigh' will cover the band's first three records that lead to the tragic disappearance of the band's chief lyricist and guitarist Richey Edwards in January 1995. Chapter Three, 'Freed from the Memory' will focus on the band's major success from 1996 to 2000 and the culture of Britpop, New Labour, and Cool Britannia that encapsulates the late 1990s. After this, Chapter Four, titled 'The Paralyzed Future' will settle on a period that included moments that many might consider an attempt by the band to redefine themselves between the years 2000 and 2007. Chapter Five, titled 'Art for the Masses' will focus on the band's second wind of success and creative re-emergence from 2007 to 2012. As a conclusion to the Manics story, we'll follow the period from 2013 to the present day with the chapter titled 'The Sense of the Familiar' This period puts the band in a retrospective mood as they revisited and reissued old records and looked back on their history as a band, yet still endeavoured to create new and interesting music.

To conclude the book, I'll offer some suggestions on which direction the Manics could go as they traverse the autumn stages of their career. It is meant to be a subjective offering, but I hope that the Manics still have some fire in their belly and some cracking records in them. The future is possible.

CHAPTER ONE
There's Work to be Done (1985-1991)

The Manic Street Preachers formed in 1985/86 in Blackwood, Wales, and forged their political leanings in the fires of political turbulence that ignited two years earlier in 1984 when British Prime Minister Margaret Thatcher declared class war on the British Mining industry. Thatcher and her cronies wanted to break up the solidarity and comradeship that existed within the Unions that represented the Miners communities and began a campaign of pit closures. In Blackwood, the mining industry had thrived for decades, but with the closures came upheaval and many miners were forced out of their good-paying lifetime jobs and went on strike to force the government's hand into retreating.

In this atmosphere of unrest, James Dean Bradfield, Sean Moore, Nicholas Jones (Nicky Wire), and Richey Edwards would form a bond that would take them from bedroom intellectuals to concert halls in a matter of years. Music, books, films, and philosophy were consumed and spat back out. Low and high cultures were discussed with equal passion. The lessons of Marx, Nietzsche, Strummer, Rotten, and later Chuck D, and Slash and Rose were learned with equal seriousness and consideration. Thoughts turned towards forming a band or at least some kind of collective that revolved around art, poetry, and expression.

The boys certainly stood out among the miners in their filthy work overalls and the other residents of Blackwood. The group of friends had taken to wearing eyeliner, leopard print blouses, and sticking their hair up with Coke in spiky punk signatures.

Their friendship formed an almost impenetrable cocoon around them as the town disintegrated from the fallout of the Miners' Strike. It is fair to say that many young people flee their dreary hometowns and look back in horror at what they left behind. The members of Manic Street Preachers were perhaps no different. Yet the Manics, through lyrics, interviews, and actions have always expressed a deep connection to their home country, the town of Blackwood, and the time they spent there as youths, and the earlier denouncements of their hometown have been replaced with later reflections of love and respect. As the text of this book unfolds, we will further explore this aspect of their career and how Welsh identity and nostalgia for home has affected their work. But for now, we are still in the grasp of youthful reactions.

In their original formation, the band consisted of Bradfield on guitar and vocals, Wire on rhythm guitar, Moore on drums, and a local bass player by the name of Miles 'Flicker' Woodward. At some point in this early incarnation Jennifer Watkins-Isnardi took on lead vocals and her account of her time in the band can be found in the book *In the Beginning: My Life with the Manic Street Preachers*. At some point, the group was reduced to the core three members. Bradfield remaining on guitar and vocals, Moore still on drums, and Wire switching from guitar to bass in replacement of an ejected Flicker. Edwards' only involvement at this point was as a rather handsome roadie, driver, and band photographer.

The first rumblings of the Manic Street Preachers music can be found in a rough collection of demos that span from 1985-1990. Chronologically this is where the band found their origins, but these demos only saw the light of day well after the band had a few records and hit singles under their belts.

The track listing is as follows.

First Demo

Faceless Sense Of Void (Early version of Love's Sweet Exile); Go Buzz Baby Go (Early Version of Motorcycle Emptiness); Just Can't Be Happy; R.P. McMurphy; Suicide Alley; New Art Riot; England is a Bitch; This Girl Got Nothing; Love in a Make-Up Bag; Generation Terrorists (Early version of Stay Beautiful); UK Channel Boredom; Sunglass Aesthetic; You Love Us; Methadone Pretty; Dying a Thousand Deaths; Eating Myself from the Inside; Democracy Coma; Repeat; Behave Yourself Baby; Repeat; Razorblade Beat; Where Have all the Good Things Gone; Whiskey Psychosis; Soul Contamination; Tennessee (I Get Low – Suicide Alley B Side, Early version of Tennessee)[1]

The demos themselves are ramshackle punk rock played at 100mph, with each member shifting gears and changing speeds throughout the recordings and never quite moving at the same jolt. Bradfield's voice howls over the top of the racket and lyrics go unheard. As a set of songs, it shows that at this point the band's sound, direction (is it jangle pop? Is it punk?) and general competency as musicians is still very much in its infancy. But there is also something quite charming and uplifting about hearing these recordings, especially in the context (as it would have been for almost every listener) of the band's massive success and musical accompaniments.

Songs that would later appear on record are here in embryonic form. Methadone Pretty, Tennessee (I Get Low), Repeat, Generation Terrorists (re-titled Stay Beautiful), Faceless Sense of Void (later known as Love's Sweet Exile) and You Love Us would all appear on the band's debut record *Generation Terrorists*. Whilst Soul Contamination, Democracy Coma, R.P. McMurphy, and UK Channel Boredom (re-tilted to Vision of Dead Desire) would be included as B-sides during the *Generation Terrorists* singles campaigns. Suicide Alley would be re-recorded for the band's debut single, whilst New Art Riot would be the lead track on the band's first EP with indie label Damaged Goods.

What is also surprising is that parts of songs would be re-used and incorporated into new songs along the way. As you can see above, Go Buzz Baby Go was an early interpretation of the band's future hit single Motorcycle Emptiness. But the rather jaunty acoustic song Behave Yourself Baby contains a short bridge that features the lyric "All we want from you is the skin you live within" which would later morph into the main bridge of Motorcycle Emptiness with a slight lyric change of "All we want from you are the kicks you've given us".

Listening to these demos it is kudos to the band that they stuck with the imprints of these songs and built version upon version until they eventually had a finished product. The musical evolution from these demos to the 1991 Heavenly single Motown Junk or the eventual beauty of Motorcycle Emptiness is extraordinary. A leap in ability and confidence that isn't seen a lot in such a short space of time.

Single 1:

Suicide Alley
Released: June 1988; UK Chart Position: n/a; Label: Self-released; Album: n/a
B-sides: Tennessee (I Get Low)
Producer: Self-produced

The first official release from Manic Street Preachers was Suicide Alley which was self-issued on 7" vinyl in June 1988. A bristling punk surge, the single was limited to 300 copies that were mostly sent out to music journalists, indie labels, and radio hosts. The cover of the single featured Bradfield, Moore, and Wire hanging tough in a Blackwood back alley. The photograph on the sleeve of the single was taken by Richey Edwards and many copies featured handwritten notes by him explaining the band's intentions of world domination and the eventual destruction of rock and roll music. The release languished for a year until *NME* journalist Steven Wells picked it up and printed a review and selected it as the magazines 'Single of the Week' in the August 1989 edition.

Extended Play 1:

New Art Riot EP
Released 22 June 1990; UK Chart Position: n/a; Label: Damaged Goods
Track Listing: New Art Riot; Strip it Down; Last Exit on Yesterday; Teenage 20/20 (lyrics by Edwards and Wire, music by Bradfield and Moore)
Producer: Robin Wynn Evans

The timing of the review could not have been better. The band, now featuring Edwards as a permanent member contributing guitar and co-writing lyrics with Wire, were scheduled to play their first London show at The Horse and Groom pub on Great Portland Street the following month. The buzz surrounding the band was in full swing and the punters who lined the walls of the small room in the Horse and Groom were mostly those attuned to the buzz. The set list for this event is included below.

Horse and Groom Set list

- New Art Riot
- Strip It Down
- Dead Yankee Drawl
- Anti-Love
- Destroy the Dancefloor
- Soul Contamination
- Repeat (UK)
- Sorrow 16
- Love's Sweet Exile
- Suicide Alley
- Tennessee

Bob Stanley, a music journalist and soon to be a member of the dream-pop band Saint Etienne was in attendance and the gig would be given a solid review in the following week's *Melody Maker*. One other individual in attendance that evening was Ian Ballad from Damaged Goods Records who took an instant liking to the band and offered them a one-off deal to record a single or EP. He sent them to Workshop Studios in Redditch and the band rattled out four songs in two days with producer Robin Wynn Evans.

The EP, titled New Art Riot, featured four songs that offered a slight evolution from the early demos and the Suicide Alley single, but its production was shambolic, and the instrumentation mistimed and shoddy. Lyrically though, the band had progressed greatly and the angry poetics that would feature as a staple of Manics future releases was evident here.

The EP begins with the song New Art Riot and its stop and start structure offers the listener an uneven listening experience but a thrilling set of lyrical couplets that singled it out as a good protest song about the stale state of the UK where "Hospital closures kill more than car bombs ever will" and where the British Government "cold shoulder insurgents yet love arms dealers".

Strip It Down, the EP's second track was perhaps the collection's most successful song in terms of sound and execution. The song rattles along at a cracking pace and simmers with anger towards the "Slicked back injustice" that "sits nicely next to smiles" of the British political establishment. The band must have thought highly of the song at the time as a music video was produced that featured the band in sloganed t-shirts playing in front of a vomit-inducing fractal backdrop. The video offers hints at the style that the band would take for the coming years of stencilling slogans like "Bomb the Past" written on cheap shirts and blouses. The jeans were white and tight as was the uniform of the Manics at this stage.

The sleeve of the EP featured a crumbled flag of the European Union and a quotation by Karl Marx which stated, "I am nothing and should be everything". Of course, the attitude of the band at this time reflected that quotation somewhat perfectly. The Manics really did want to be 'everything' to everyone and conquer all, but at this point, they were (if, not quite) 'nothing' in terms of record sales, sold-out shows, and fan devotion. Only a few indie label heads, fanzine writers, and music journalists had clocked on to the band's genius. Most music listeners were nonplussed. New Art Riot wouldn't really change this perception, but it was reviewed well and the EP fell into the top 100 of the UK single charts and would propel the band towards more features and interviews in the weekly music magazines.

Damaged Goods optioned another single, but with the press and general buzz surrounding the band increasing, a larger label with better distribution was needed. The Manics parted ways with Damaged Goods on undamaged terms. In came Creation Records alumnus Jeff Barrett who had recently set up his own independent label Heavenly Records. Heavenly had released singles by dream-pop band Saint Etienne and indie dance band Flowered Up. The thought of having punk provocateurs Manic Street Preachers signed up was puzzling. But it offered the band some legitimacy among the naysayers who saw the band at this point as kids playing at being The Clash in a school play.

Single 2:
Motown Junk (lyrics by Edwards and Wire, music by Bradfield and Moore) Released 21st January 1991; UK Chart Position: 94; Label: Heavenly; Album: n/a

B-sides: Sorrow 16; We Her Majesty's Prisoners
(lyrics by Edwards and Wire, music by Bradfield
and Moore)
Producer: Robin Wynn Evans

The first release for Heavenly Records was
Motown Junk, issued on 21st January 1991. The song
stood as really the first in the band's arsenal that set
out a proper agenda. A mini-manifesto of indent and
purpose. Via a Public Enemy sample that kicks off the
song, Motown Junk called for "Revolution,
Revolution" and went on to summarize the band's
past of growing up and escaping from the "pissed
towns" where being "adrift in cheap dreams don't
stop the rain" and where the only thing going for
them was "the boredom I suffocate in". Motown Junk
was also a reactionary song against the current
cultural climate of overproduced and smooth
interpretations of soul and pop music (hence the
junk) that "Stops your brain thinking for 168
seconds".
        But the song also established a reaction
against the worship of false idols, claiming in the
song's most notorious refrain that "I laughed when
Lennon got shot". This line was a somewhat shocking
and controversial statement as Lennon was still
idolized by many and his re-emergence in the public
sphere was only a few years away with the arrival of
Oasis and that band's worship of The Beatles and
Lennon and McCartney in particular. Those lyrics did
not last long in the live setting.
Motown Junk ends with a statement of intent with
Bradfield proclaiming that "we live in urban hell we
destroy rock and roll." It was always the band's
intention to muddy the waters of music's

complacency. Destroying rock and roll by remaking it and grafting intelligent lyrics to bright and bouncy punk rock was the agenda they set early on.

Motown Junk was recorded at The Power Plant studies with producer Robin Evans. Much like the recording of New Art Riot, the band skipped through the session in two days, but this time around the results did not feel rushed. It was just a real rush of adrenaline to listen to.

The single came in an iconic sleeve. A picture of a crisped and burnt pocket watch stopped at the exact moment the Hiroshima bomb had detonated. Motown Junk felt like the image. A visual representation of being blasted with energy and light.

Along the way to signing to Heavenly Records, the band picked up a manager, Philip Hall of the public relations office Hall or Nothing. Hall had been a journalist for Record Mirror, a music weekly for record collectors. In the mid-1980s, Hall was then recruited by the indie label Stiff Records, home to Ian Dury and The Pogues. He had then launched an independent PR business. Hall took an instant liking to the members and as well as providing PR services for the band he became their manager and a parental figure as the young band navigated the music industry. It was Hall who pushed the Manics to sign with Heavenly, and Bradfield, in an interview with *The Quietus* recalls that Hall "made it very clear to us that we needed Heavenly much more than Heavenly needed us. And the bottom line is that because that record was on Heavenly, people who were in two minds about us were prepared to give us a second look."[2]

And a second look they got. Motown Junk pierced the Top 100 and according to Wire "sold out every week" and "stayed at 92 for four weeks."[3]

The single was backed by Sorrow 16 and We Her Majesty's Prisoners. Sorrow 16 had been a regular in the band's live sets and the version present on Motown Junk is pleasant enough. We Her Majesty's Prisoners is perhaps the most interesting song of the two. Originally titled Ceremonial Rape Machine, Heavenly rejected the title and demanded it was renamed for release. The song has an air of epic breeziness under its fuzzy production and the inclusion of some lovely plinking piano adds further weight to this feeling.

All in all, Motown Junk would be a torchbearer for things to come. A short and punchy stab of punk rock that infused all the band's frustrations, hopes, and intentions in one atomic blast. The song remains a highlight of the band's live set list to this day. Rubbing up awkwardly against the epic scope of songs like Design for Life and If You Tolerate This Your Children Will Be Next. Arguably songs that Motown Junk denounced.

The video for the song was an edited collection of live footage that showed the excitement of a Manics live show circa '91 but did not really convey the overall intelligence and drama of the band. That was still to come.

Single 3:

You Love Us (Heavenly Version) [lyrics by Edwards and Wire, music by Bradfield and Moore]
Released: 7th May 1991; UK Chart Position: 62;
Label: Heavenly; Album: n/a
B-sides: Spectators of Suicide; Starlover; Strip it Down (Live at Bath Moles) [lyrics by Edwards and Wire, music by Bradfield and Moore]
Producer: Robin Wynn Evans

Heavenly and the Manic Street Preachers still had business to attend to. The label sent the band, alongside label mates Saint Etienne and Flowered Up on a package tour of the UK and Europe. And a second single was already in the bag and awaiting release.

Released on 7th May 1991, You Love Us was considered a tongue in cheek two-finger salute to the band's naysayers in the music press. The same figures who slagged them off for being a flash in the pan yet still wrote up reviews and printed interviews knowing the band's controversy was selling magazines, pulling in readers, and turning those readers into fans.

Like Motown Junk, You Love Us set out another punk rock mini-statement of intent telling the muso-journalists that "we are not your sinners" and that the band's "voices are for real" An accusation that the band had often had pointed at them by the music press and that the band "can never belong" to them or anyone other than themselves.

4 Real

When questioned about the band's punk rock legitimacy by *NME* journalist Steve Lamacq after a gig at the Norwich Arts Centre on 15th May 1991, Richey Edwards quietly explained the passion and seriousness of the band's intentions whilst simultaneously slicing "4 Real" into his forearm with a razor blade he happened to be carrying with him.

The gruesome photo captured moments after of Edwards clutching his arm whilst staring down the camera with a slight smirk on his face has since become iconic, if deeply disturbing in the context of what we now know of Edwards' mental health and self-harm issues. The image caused quite a stir and many in the music press were conflicted about printing it in full colour or not, citing that many readers might follow suit or feel justified in harming themselves. The whole episode is brilliantly captured on the audio documentary Sleeping with The NME which featured as a B-side to the band's 1992 charity single Theme from M.A.S.H. (Suicide Is Painless).

You Love Us was also a type of song that would become familiar to fans of the band as time went on: a song about being a Manic Street Preacher. The "us" in the lyric is not aimed at a subculture but right at the feet of the band themselves. Whilst You Love Us spoke to the listener on this level it was also one of the most political. In a modern context, one can't help but hear a lyric like "'til I see love in statues / your lessons drill inherited sin" as a forebear to the recent removal (voluntary or not) of statues and monuments across the globe that have commemorated people, places and events that no longer gel with our current version or interpretation of history, or the future we want. The "inherited sin" of slave traders and racist leaders has been jettisoned.

     The song begins with a sampled scream of strings from Krzysztof Penderecki's Threnody to the Victims of Hiroshima, a call back to the Motown Junk sleeve art of the Hiroshima watch. If this starter sample seemed obtuse and highbrow, then the drum sample of Iggy Pop's Lust for Life that acts as the song's coda is the cultural flipside. As the drums swagger on, Bradfield bellows "Hey passive electorate / Die die die".

     The video that accompanied You Love Us was a more successful promotion of the band's aesthetics and excitement than Motown Junk. It featured the band in knowing rock and roll poses from the studio to the interspersed live footage. Star kicks, guitar licks, pouting lips, and swinging hips, the video is the most exquisite of the band's early work.

Whilst the song You Love Us continued the punk rock audio assault that had started with Suicide Alley and carried on to New Art Riot EP and Motown Junk, a small surprise lay on the B-side. Spectators of Suicide saw the Manics slowing down the tempo if not the attitude and it made for a successfully effortless sense of cool that currently was not in the band's arsenal. Under the fuzz of guitar, the song begins with a sample of a speech made by Black Panther Party co-founder Robert Seale proclaiming in no uncertain terms that "we're going to walk on this nation. We're going to walk on this racist power structure. And we're going to say to the whole damn government: 'Stick 'em up motherfucker, this is a hold-up! We've come for what's ours!"[4]. As the drums launch the song, a piano carries the guitar notes higher and Bradfield's voice becomes a detached sleepy drawl. Though not one of Bradfield's most stunning vocal turns, the performance suits the deflated mood of the piece where "the only free choice is the refusal to pay" in reaction to living in modern capitalist society. Spectators of Suicide becomes a kind of mini rock-opera and a song that certainly would not have been associated with the early punk rock raggers of early Manic Street Preachers. Yet here it is, and in some ways, it points in the direction of more mournful epics like Motorcycle Emptiness and Little Baby Nothing that were just on the band's horizon.

Both You Love Us and Spectators of Suicide, for good or ill, would be re-recorded for the band's

24

debut record. The album versions would become the definitive renditions for many. You Love Us would turn up the bass and drums and become a heavier metal standard that dropped the high/low cultural references and instead riffed its way in and out. Spectators of Suicide was perhaps the biggest difference and the most bizarre. The track was given an acoustic overhaul and the original effortless cool was replaced with something more debauched that might have sat comfortably on the back half of Guns N' Roses' 1988 record *G N' R Lies.* Nicky Wire has often stated he felt like the album version is similar to The Lion Sleeps Tonight, which was never intended as a compliment.

But it is worth pausing and reflecting on the quality of You Love Us and Spectators of Suicide and the Heavenly Recordings as a whole. These recordings mark a significant stepping stone in the band's evolution to what would become a startling career. In an interview with *The Quietus,* Nicky Wire remarked that "If there's one regret I have about the band is, if only we could have done a mini-album on Heavenly. "[5]

Of course one could take all the recordings made with Heavenly and order them together into a coherent min-album, but the truth remains that the leap from punk rock provocateurs on a little indie label to a sprawling eighteen track debut rock album of debauched and whisky-soaked anthems that came in early 1992 is quite massive and somewhat impressive. A little stop-gap to show the progress might have gone some way as a primer towards the colossal debut record that would be *Generation Terrorists.*

CHAPTER TWO
Scream to a Sigh (1992-1995)

The buzz surrounding the band after the release of
Motown Junk and You Love Us was increasing by the
day and their continued feature in the weekly music
press became common. It was clear that Heavenly
Records was too small a home for the band's
ambitions of world dominance. It was always a naive
dream, but the band had set the goal to become a
world-famous rock act within the first few years of
existence. The story changes from source to source,
but the lead goal for the band was to sell sixteen
million copies of their debut record, play a few sold-
out shows at Wembley Arena and then either blow
themselves up on stage or disband in some other
outrageous fashion. Either way, one absolutely era-
defining rock and roll double record was always the
band's goal. This record would become a final
statement that would change or destroy all music
that came after it. To say the band placed huge
pressure on themselves to see this record through
was somewhat of an understatement.

Though some people did believe it was
possible. Rob Stringer, an executive with Columbia
Records, a subsidiary of Sony Music, saw enough
potential to sign the band for a record deal worth
£250,0000. This was a substantial amount for a band
that had yet to have a top 40 hit and were still playing
dirty backrooms of pubs and small venues as
supporting acts.

To put this into some context, it is worth
taking a minute to consider the huge cultural shift
that has taken place over the past three decades in

which Manic Street Preachers first proclaimed world domination or bust. Sixteen million sold records and a handful of sell-out shows at Wembley Stadium was at this time in 1991/92 the pinnacle of success. Today, this might seem ambitious but totally achievable not through sales per see, but via streams on apps such as Spotify, iTunes, and YouTube. Sixteen million is today a small(ish) number when one considers recording artists like the intolerable Ed Sheeran has had, at the time of writing, six billion plus plays on Spotify. During the year 2017, Sheeran maintained his vice-like grip on the streaming charts, becoming the most-streamed artist every single month, apart from January of that year. Canadian rap artist Drake achieved over eight billion streams in 2019 alone and remains the most streamed artist since digital music streams began being logged. It is quite extraordinary that artists now consider record sales secondary to streaming when the form is still in its infancy and many new artists, or smaller acts, simply cannot rely on the quite shameful royalty percentage that Spotify and iTunes dish out to artists. Only those in the millions and billions of streams can really earn from this format. And these plays have to remain consistent.

Manic Street Preachers would struggle to establish themselves as a formidable act if starting out in today's market. Their biggest hit, 1998's If You Tolerate This Your Children Will Be Next, stands at a respectable 38,131,124 streams on Spotify.[6] It's a big number and far outstrips their initial prediction to sell sixteen million records. But in today's market, the figure is comparatively low and bands like Manic Street Preachers still rely on physical record sales and live performances to achieve a living.

In the Summer of 1991, Columbia Records packed the band off to Black Barn Studios in London with producer Steve Brown. Working under the manifest title of Culture, Alienation, Boredom & Despair, the band's debut album would become a massive eighteen track monolith that clocked in at over seventy-three minutes and took twenty-three weeks to complete. The record shifts in lyrical themes from the political to the personal and sometimes combining both.

Generation Terrorists

<u>Single 4:</u>

Stay Beautiful (lyrics by Edwards and Wire, music by Bradfield and Moore)
Released: 29th July 1991, UK Chart Position: 40:
Label: Columbia; Album: *Generation Terrorists*
B-sides: R.P. McMurphy; Soul Contamination (lyrics by Edwards and Wire, music by Bradfield and Moore)
Producer: Steve Brown

To prepare the public for their forthcoming mainstream arrival, the single Stay Beautiful, released on 29th July 1991, would also become the band's first hit, entering the top 40 at number 40. The song had been a part of the band's live set for a short time and its memorable chorus refrain of "why don't you just fuck off" was an early crowd-pleaser. However, to guarantee some radio exposure, the "fuck off" line was replaced by a squeal of Bradfield guitar. Audiences throughout the Manics' live performances have ensured that the original line remains always present and joyfully shouted at the top of the lungs.

Stay Beautiful was an obvious choice for an early single. It could have sat quite comfortably as a Heavenly release and bridges the gap between indie cred and major-label release. The song bops along on a melody of melancholia and informs the listener that the band is "a mess of eyeliner and spray paint" whilst simultaneously tut-tutting at the listener for filling their heads with "broken heroes" and "lonely wreckage". The song ends on the repeated refrain of "Destroyed by madness" echoing Allen Ginsberg's opening line of his famous poem Howl which reads "I saw the best minds of my generation destroyed by madness"[7]

To keep the momentum in place, the song Love's Sweet Exile along with Repeat U.K was released as a double A-side single on 28 October 1991. Both songs had been knocking around in various forms for years, but it was a neat way for the band to show listeners how the new record was progressing and how different it could potentially be.

Single 5:

Love's Sweet Exile (lyrics by Edwards and Wire, music by Bradfield and Moore)
Released: 28th October 1991; UK Chart Position: 26: Label: Columbia; Album *Generation Terrorists*
B-sides: Repeat (UK); Democracy Coma (lyrics by Edwards and Wire, music by Bradfield and Moore)
Producer: Steve Brown.

Love's Sweet Exile had mutated from its life as the punky Faceless Sense of Void to a more metal incarnation. The drums pounded whilst the guitars grated against Bradfield's shouty delivery. Repeat U.K on the other hand still harkened back to the band's more punk rock roots and maintained its blistering assault on "Queen and country". Love's Sweet Exile led the two with an exquisite monochrome promotional video directed by Andrew John "W.I.Z." Whistonwhich who would go on to direct future Manics videos as well as for acts like Marylyn Manson and Kasabian.

The homoerotism was turned up to eleven with all members (bar Sean Moore, who opted for a Batman mask) withering around nude on the floor and against each other. The video began with a quotation from Albert Camus which reads "And then came human beings. They wanted to cling, but there was nothing to cling to." Famously, the band would make a switch at the last minute as musical guests on the late-night youth program *The Word*. Instead of performing the safer Love's Sweet Exile, they launched into the anti-royal tirade of Repeat U.K and then trashed the studio. Love's Sweet Exile reached number 26 in the British single charts. Alongside the main two tracks of the single release, Democracy Coma, a song we saw way back on the early demo tapes, sat as a re-recorded B-side.

Single 6:

You Love Us (lyrics by Edwards and Wire, music by Bradfield and Moore)
Released: 16 January 1992, UK Chart Position: 16, Label: Columbia; Album: *Generation Terrorists* B-sides: A Vision of Dead Desire; We Her Majesty's Prisoners; It's So Easy (Live at London Marquee)

[lyrics by Edwards and Wire, music by Bradfield and Moore]
Producer: Steve Brown

As a final prelude to the release of the mother album, the re-recorded version of You Love Us was issued on 16 January 1992. As previously discussed, the album version was a more metallic incarnation which saw the samples dropped in favour of a Bradfield riff. By 1 February, the song had reached number sixteen in the UK Official Singles Charts. The single was backed by the Heavenly version of We Her Majesty's Prisoners as well as A Vision of Dead Desire and a live rendition of Guns N' Roses It's So Easy recorded at London's Marquee venue on 4 September 1991. The G N' R cover was perhaps a good indicator of the sound the Manics were now attempting to replicate. For years the debate within the band had been whether or not to sign up to the indie ethos of band's like McCarthy who had always subscribed to a socialist worldview but had wallowed in relative indie obscurity or to sneak in politically charged lyrics, Trojan horse style, to face-melting riffs and banging drums and become a massive band. The inclusion of It's So Easy was perhaps the answer to this debate. Although it would continue to be debated continuously over the coming decades.

With already four tracks in the bag as singles and an increasing audience, *Generation Terrorists* was released on 10 February 1992 and entered the charts at a respectable number 13. It would have cracked the top ten any other week, except the annual Brit Award winners had benefited from their awarded trophies and rose up the charts in front of them. The track listing for the record stretched to eighteen tracks and was issued in the UK as below.

<u>Album 1:</u>

Generation Terrorists
Released: 10th February 1992; UK Chart Position: 13; Label: Columbia Records
Track Listing: Slash 'N' Burn; Nat West-Barclays-Midlands-Lloyds; Born to End; Motorcycle Emptiness; You Love Us; Love's Sweet Exile; Little Baby Nothing; Repeat; Tennessee; Another Invented Disease; Stay Beautiful; So Dead; Repeat; Spectators of Suicide; Damn Dog; Crucifix Kiss; Methadone Pretty; Condemned to Rock 'N' Roll (lyrics by Edwards and Wire, music by Bradfield and Moore)
Producer: Steve Brown

For this short and concise text, a full and descriptive assessment of the record would potentially fill the remainder of the book and then some. Suffice to say that *Generation Terrorists* is the Manic Street Preachers' biggest rock beast. Despite its length, there are only a handful of duds that could have been omitted for time's sake. The short and pointless Damn Dog, Tennessee, Spectators of Suicide (although the Heavenly version would have been welcome) could have been jettisoned, but this would leave it a lesser record. *Generation Terrorists* requires its weaker tracks to complement its highs.

And what highs. The first seven tracks are stellar rock anthems. The run is only interrupted by Repeat (Stars and Stripes), the Bomb Squad remix of Repeat U.K. The song might have benefited if it had sat as an oddity on a B-side to one of the *Generation Terrorists* singles, but having it here, and before the actual original version of Repeat seems to indicate it as pure filler. Tennessee is another fairly week song, a remnant of the band's early works, but the album launches off again with Another Invented Disease and only stalls at Spectators of Suicide and Damn Dog, before closing on a solid trifecta of songs.

Within this mess of Culture, Alienation, Boredom, and Despair, sat some real gems. Motorcycle Emptiness was an obvious standout, and as it was issued as a single some months after the record's release, we will discuss it more in-depth at a later point.

Little Baby Nothing, a duet with porn actress Tracey Lords, might have pushed the boundaries of what was acceptable for a punk rock band, but the song's lovely melody (plagiarised from their own Suicide Alley) and Lord's exquisite bubble-gum vocal added to the decadent feel of the song.

Both Motorcycle Emptiness and Little Baby Nothing would become singles, but it is perhaps the album's last three tracks that have in my opinion become the album's defining moments, ones that summarize the contents and remain a testament to the strength of the band's debut collection. The fact that at this point in an already exceptionally long record there is still surprise and excitement to be found is admirable. Crucifix Kiss, Methadone Pretty, and Condemned to Rock 'n' Roll offer the political commentary and societal alienation in a more pinpointed sense. If, in some twisted reality, *Generation Terrorists* had been the band's final statement then closing the book fully with Condemned to Rock 'n' Roll would have been a masterstroke. The track oozes heroin-chic decadence and reeks of cheap whiskey and cigarette smoke. The glacial pace of the track emphasizes the weariness and burn out of rock and roll excess and ends on the quite haunting lyric "there's nowhere I wanna go / there's nothing I wanna see".

This was not the reality of the band at all. Apart from the consumption of booze and cigs, the members of the band were drug-free and Nicky Wire even went teetotal during this period of time. Whilst bands such as The Happy Mondays, Primal Scream, and Depeche Mode popped, injected, and snorted through mountains of ecstasy, heroin, and coke, the Manics lived an almost monastic lifestyle in comparison to those hedonists. Yet, the mythology surrounding rock's forebears, the Jim's, Jimmy's, and Janice's of lore, was something the Manics brought into wholesale and sold back to their audience.

Of course, in time the band would be associated with these characters along with more recent additions such as Ian Curtis and Kurt Cobain for different reasons. But for now, *Generation Terrorists* and the era that surrounds it was the Manics at their most pure at heart. There would not be many more opportunities over the decades that saw them this innocent and in such belief of their own vision. The band's upward trajectory meant they had not yet faced many setbacks or learned many lessons.

<u>Single 7:</u>

Slash 'n' Burn (lyrics by Edwards and Wire, music by Bradfield and Moore)
Released: 16 March 1992; UK Chart Position: 20;
Label: Columbia; Album; *Generation Terrorists*

B-sides: Motown Junk; Sorrow 16; Ain't Going
Down (lyrics by Edwards and Wire, music by
Bradfield and Moore)
Producer: Steve Brown

With the record performing well, thoughts
turned towards more single releases. The first single
to be issued after the record's release was the
muscular anthem Slash N' Burn, a track that also
opened the record. The song's anti-capitalist stance
was one of the more successful in the band's current
arsenal of political songs that matched the lyrics with
a heavy set of riffs and drums. In effect, sneaking the
ethos of the band's anti-capitalist stance under the
radar. The single release was backed with the
Heavenly single Motown Junk and Sorrow 16 and
Ain't Going Down. The single peaked at number 20 in
the UK Official Singles Chart.

Single 8:

Motorcycle Emptiness (lyrics by Edwards and
Wire, music by Bradfield and Moore)
Released: 1 June 1992; UK Chart Position: 17;
Label: Columbia; Album: *Generation Terrorists*
B-sides: Bored Out of My Mind; Crucifix Kiss (live);
Under My Wheels (live) [lyrics by Edwards and
Wire, music by Bradfield and Moore]
Producer: Steve Brown

Finally, on 1 June 1992, the band decided to
grace the world with the elegant Motorcycle
Emptiness as a single release. The song was a
composite of earlier demos and the eventual outcome

would become one of the band's most loved and most performed. Almost everything about the song has an air of perfection. From the sad and yearning vocal delivery, the drums that glide and hover, the lyrics that confront consumerism, the underscore of plucked strings that give the track a moving, almost cinematic quality. Even the accompanying music video, which was filmed on the streets of Tokyo, Japan seems to perfectly reflect the "neon loneliness" and the "wonderful world of purchase power" of the song, as Bradfield, wearing a suit and shades, stands motionless among the hustling crowds of Tokyo. The single charted at number seventeen in the UK and stayed there again the following week.

The song even clocked top forty status in Belgium, Netherlands, and New Zealand.
With decent radio play, an atmospheric performance on *Top of the Pops*, and rotation on *MTV*, Motorcycle Emptiness perhaps should have charted higher, maybe smashing the Top Ten. But it would be the band's next single, a cover of Johnny Mandel and Mike Altman's Suicide Is Painless that would rocket the band into the Top Ten and leave them there for a three-week period.

Suicide Is Painless was recorded in a one-day session for £80 in Cardiff's Sound Space Studios, to commemorate the *NME*'s fortieth anniversary of publication, and featured on a triple album titled *Ruby Trax - The NME's Roaring Forty*. Among the Manics contribution, Blur delivered a cover of Maggie May by the Small Faces, Teenage Fanclub covered Bob Dylan's Mr. Tambourine Man, and Suede put in a saucy rendition of Brass in Pocket by The Pretenders. All proceeds from the album and single were donated to the National Spastics Society, now known as Scope.

Single 9:

Theme from M.A.S.H. (Suicide is Painless) [Johnny Mandel and Mike Altman]
Released: 7th September 1992; UK Chart Position: 7; Label: Columbia: Album: *Ruby Trax – The NME's Roaring Forty*
B-sides: (Everything I Do) I Do It for You, by Fatima Mansions [Bryan Adams, Michael Kamen Robert John 'Mutt' Lange]; Sleeping with the N.M.E. (lyrics by Edwards and Wire, music by Bradfield and Moore)
Producer: Self-Produced

The song, rather than the band, had something to do with the massive success. Originally written for the film adaptation of the hit American show *M.A.S.H*, the lyrics were thought up by Mike Altman, *M.A.S.H*'s director Robert Altman's fourteen-year-old son in five minutes. Never say that the mind of a teenager cannot quantify teen angst. The lyrical content of the song remains incomparably sad. The song suited the Manics, but stripped of their political thunder and not coming from the band's current record, *Generation Terrorists,* Suicide Is Painless would be a hollow victory, but one the band nevertheless would fully embrace and build upon.

The last single to be released from *Generation Terrorists* would be Little Baby Nothing on 16 November 1992. The song, a duet with Traci Lords, would be a final stab to send the mother album in the stratosphere. The single peaked at number 29 in the single charts. It has since become a fan favourite. Though rarely played live, the song has become a kind of mini-manifesto of the Manic Street Preachers experience. The line sung by Lords in which she laments "culture, alienation, boredom, and despair" not only summarizes *Generation Terrorists* as a record, but the whole ethos of the band going forward.

Single 10:

Little Baby Nothing (lyrics by Edwards and Wire, music by Bradfield and Moore)
Released: 16 November 1992; UK Chart Position: 29; Label: Columbia: Album: *Generation Terrorists*
B-sides: Dead Yankee Drawl; Suicide Alley; Never Want Again; R.P. McMurphy (Live); Tennessee (Live); You Love Us (Live) [lyrics by Edwards and Wire, music by Bradfield and Moore]
Producer: Steve Brown

Generation Terrorists did not set the world aflame as was promised. It did not sell in its millions or destroy music as it was intended. But what was remarkable about the record was the year-long campaign that saw the band chart seven singles in the Top Forty and make appearances on television and radio. From late-night youth television shows like *The Word.* to early morning children's shows such as *Gimme 5*. They appeared on the Tommy Vance Rock Show and the Radio One Roadshow. For almost a solid year, the Manics infected the nation with political proto-metal/glam punk anthems that would seep into the collective conscience. Eventually anyway. It was quite the feat.

Learning a few lessons from the *Generation Terrorists* era, the band continued into 1993 with a few changes. Firstly, the colour and vibrancy of their punk rock aesthetics had to be scaled back. Feather boas and leopard print coats were decommissioned in favour of pinstripe suits and facial stubble. To be fair the metamorphosis had begun in the later stages of the *Generation Terrorists* era. What also had to be tossed aside was the flashy political slogans of the lyrics. By 1993, the sub-genre of Grunge had conquered the world. Pearl Jam, Nirvana, Soundgarden, and Alice in Chains fused metal and punk riffs with sombre lyrics that reflected a more personal and introverted perspective. Politics was still apparent in these bands, but the lyrical concern seemed to fall on the hardships of the soul brought on by society's ills. The Manics political messaging fell mostly on deaf ears and judging by their biggest hit so far, the sombre Suicide Is Painless, introversion was key to a bigger share of the pie.

Gold Against the Soul

<u>Single 11:</u>

From Despair to Where (lyrics by Edwards and Wire, music by Bradfield and Moore)
Released: 7 June 1993; UK Chart Position: 25; Label: Columbia; Album: *Gold Against the Soul*
B-sides: Hibernation; Spectators of Suicide (Heavenly Version); Starlover (Heavenly Version) [lyrics by Edwards and Wire, music by Bradfield and Moore]
Producer: David Eringa

The Band's next record, *Gold Against the Soul* would be a different beast. This was apparent with the release of the first single from the record, From

Despair to Where, which was released on 7 June 1993. The introspective and disillusioned nature of the song was obvious from the very first line of "I write this alone in my bed". The song then continues with the many personal tragedies and the "imitation of dignity" the author faces in the pursuit of living an ordinary life within modern society. The single entered the UK Official Singles Chart at number twenty-five.

The mothership album, *Gold Against the Soul* would be Released on 21 June 1993 and smash the top ten by entering in at number eight.

The record was certainly a more sombre affair and also far easier to digest. A look at the record's track listing would offer enough clues that the band was in a more introverted mood.

Album 2:

Gold Against the Soul
Released: 21st June 1993; UK Chart Position: 8; Label: Columbia
Track Listing: Sleepflower; From Despair to Where; La Tristesse Durera; Yourself; Life Becoming a Landslide; Drug Drug Druggy; Roses in the Hospital; Nostalgic Pushead; Symphony of Tourette; Gold Against the Soul (lyrics by Edwards and Wire, music by Bradfield and Moore)
Producer: Dave Eringa

Gone were the political polemics in title form alone, *Gold Against the Soul* offered more a reflection of the sadness of living in the modern age. The first three songs alone offer a bitter pill to swallow. *Gold Against the Soul* was also a more compact offering. A slim ten tracks in comparison to *Generations Terrorists* gargantuan eighteen.

Lyrically, the album was more poetic in its language and images. Songs seemed to have a theme and stay with it as opposed to what had come before.

Musically, the record has a massive step ahead. Ditching the punkier and glam rock aspects of their core sound and maintaining a more traditional rock and metal approach seemed wise in the era of Grunge music. Grunge had ended the hair metal and glam craze of the 1980s. The Manics had always seemed out of step with the burgeoning era of earnest young men in plaid shirts and cut-off combat shorts singing about personal traumas. The Manics decided on a more palatable version of themselves to accommodate the listener. Musically speaking, *Gold Against the Soul* shared more with Alice in Chains than Anarchy in The U.K.

<u>Single 12:</u>

La Tristesse Durera (Scream to a Sigh) [lyrics by Edwards and Wire, music by Bradfield and Moore]
Released: 26 July 1993; UK Chart Position: 22;
Label Columbia; Album: *Gold Against the Soul*
B-sides: Patrick Bateman; What's My Name (Live); Slash 'n' Burn (Live); Repeat (Live); Tennessee (I Get Low) [lyrics by Edwards and Wire, music by Bradfield and Moore]
Producer: Dave Eringa

I would not write off *Gold Against the Soul* as an unimpressive record. Sleepflower alone is worth its weight in...err, gold. But there is something telling about the reaction to the album in retrospect. Whilst mostly still loved by fans, the band has continued to have a different relationship with the record. It is not one of regret or of dislike (we will come on to those records in due course), but just the inoffensive nature of the record. In a piece for *Vice.com*, James Dean Bradfield remarked that *Gold Against the Soul* felt like "a classic second album" in that the band had "lost some direction" and "become a bit too rockist, a bit too bloated in our stance"[8] The record feels tired in places and lacks the energetic gusto of *Generation Terrorists*.

This is reflected in the lyrics to songs like Sleepflower ("Morning always feels too stale to justify"), From Despair to Where ("I write this alone in my bed") La Tristesse Durera (Scream to a Sigh) ("Oh, the sadness will never go"), Roses in The Hospital ("Nothing really makes me happy"). Whilst in the past the band might have coupled lines like this with a knowledge that society is the problem for feeling this way, here it is only the author's own internal mind-set that is the root cause of the issue.

The singles that the band issued from *Gold Against the Soul*, starting with From Despair to Where and then following up with La Tristesse Durera (Scream to a Sigh), Roses in The Hospital, and Life Becoming a Landslide offer a stretch of unbelievably good quality releases and should have seen the band's fortunes grow much more and far wider. They kind of did, but also kind of didn't. The band was asked to play a support slot for Bon Jovi at the Milton Keynes Bowl on September 18th, 1993. It was a chance to direct their more mature sound to the relatively middle of the road Jovi sect. Nicky Wire in an interview with *Raw* a few days before the support slot stated that the intention of playing such a massive concert was to "play music to people who hadn't heard us before, that was the whole point."[9]

From the set list of the supporting slot it was clear the band was playing it safe, but the inclusion of Repeat (UK), Motown Junk and You Love Us, at least indicated that the band was willing to engage the Jovi audience on their own terms.

Single 13:

Roses in The Hospital (lyrics by Edwards and Wire, music by Bradfield and Moore)
Released: 20 September 1993; UK Chart Position: 15; Label: Epic; Album: *Gold Against the Soul*
B-sides: Us Against You; Donkeys; Wrote for Luck (lyrics by Edwards and Wire, music by Bradfield and Moore)
Producer: Dave Eringa

Interestingly, and despite the flack they got for selling out their punk rock ethos, nearly three decades later, a very different Manic Street Preachers would join Bon Jovi again as a support act for their show at Wembley Stadium on June 21, 2019.

As the *Gold Against the Soul* era wound down the band released one final single from the record. Life Becoming a Landslide came out on February 7th and charted at number thirty-seven. The song was an emotive plea for a more innocent time. The lyrics dealt with the innocence of childhood and a "glimpse of pornography" that sets the decay towards the disillusionment of adulthood. The song offers a striking vocal performance from Bradfield as he gently emotes the first verse that morphs towards a deeper and darker growl. By the song's end, the screams of "Just a finely tuned jealousy" bust the lungs as the song rages on. Whilst Life Becoming a Landslide was a brilliant song and single release, what was more interesting was the song Comfort Comes that was nestled away as a B-side. Sounding unlike anything that the band had recorded before, the song's production was compressed, tight, and almost militant in its rigor. It certainly sounded bizarre among the epic scope of *Gold Against the Soul*'s more operatic moments.

<u>Extended Play 2:</u>

Life Becoming a Landslide
Released: 7th February 1994; UK Chart Position: 36; Label: Epic; Album; *Gold Against the Soul* Track Listing: Life Becoming a Landslide; Comfort Comes; Are Mothers Saints; Charles Windsor (lyrics by Edwards and Wire, music by Bradfield and Moore) Producer: Dave Eringa

---

Now, in retrospect, Comfort Comes makes perfect sense as a bridge towards what would become the Manics' third record. The compact sound produced in Comfort Comes would be replicated for *The Holy Bible*. But, at this point in the band's narrative, I feel we need to pause and reflect on the climate that pushed the band towards making an album like *The Holy Bible.*

As 1993 gave way to 1994, British music was changing drastically. A young indie band, consisting of a bunch of Beatles obsessed working-class Manchester lads, called Oasis were setting the stage for what would become one of the stellar moments in popular music, not just in the UK, but around the world. Britpop, a loose term coined to market the current crop of British bands that were reacting against the Americanization of music and culture in the UK, was in full swing. Blur had released two well-received records, *Leisure* in 1991 and Modern *Life Is Rubbish* in 1993. The band Suede had become the darlings of the British music scene with the release of their eponymous debut record in March 1993. Pulp, a band that had been kicking about since the early 1980s, had scored with their fourth album *His 'n' Hers* upon release on 18 April 1994 and would become a sensation the following year with the follow-up *Different Class.* Oasis's debut *Definitely Maybe* was on the horizon and they would score hit singles with Supersonic, Shakermaker, and Live Forever in the run-up to that mega album's release. Alongside the big four Britpop bands of Blur, Oasis, Pulp and Suede arose an army of other acts that rode the coattails of Britpop towards moderate success. Elastica, The Bluetones, Menswear, Sleeper, Dodgy, and Supergrass all became sensations. So where were the Manics in all of this?

The same late august week that Oasis' *Definitely Maybe* was released the Manic Street Preachers unleashed their third record *The Holy Bible.* The two records were as different from one another as chalk and cheese. Whilst Oasis sang about wanting to "live forever" and "feeling supersonic", The Manics wanted to "die in the summertime" and ask and respond in no uncertain terms "who's responsible? You fucking are". With *The Holy Bible,* the Manics had turned their anger and frustrations seen on *Generation Terrorists* and *Gold Against the Soul* into an almost apocalyptic vision of humanity. A vision that was hardly shared by the larkishness of the current crop of "mad for it" bands and artists. The

Manics had often stood apart and stood against the popular tide in music and culture, but in this case and from the relative safety of *Gold Against the Soul*, *The Holy Bible* felt utterly suffocating.

As explained in this book's introduction, Manic Street Preachers have come under intense scrutiny in books, fanzines, and podcasts. *The Holy Bible* is the epitome of this scrutiny. The book *Triptych: Three Studies of The Holy Bible* features three separate authors who take three impressive deep dives into the record's music, lyrics, artwork, and surrounding cultural artefacts. A few years later, author David Evans wrote a slim, but professionally researched and concise edition for Bloomsbury's popular 33 ⅓ series of books on the nature of the record. Researcher Yusef Sayed has been posting impressively in-depth essays on aspects of *The Holy Bible* on the website 227lears.com. What more can be said about this record? This text cannot match the levels of peeling back the layers the record offers but let us dive in anyway.

The Holy Bible

> **<u>Single 14:</u>**
>
> Faster (lyrics by Edwards and Wire, music by Bradfield and Moore)
> Released: 6th June 1994; UK Chart Position: 16; Label: Epic; Album: *The Holy Bible*
> B-sides: PCP; Sculpture of Man; New Art Riot (In E Minor) [lyrics by Edwards and Wire, music by Bradfield and Moore]
> Producer: Self-produced with Sound Engineer Alex Silva

The first release from *The Holy Bible* was the double A-side single of Faster/PCP, released on 6 June 1994. If you as a listener had been inclined towards the smoother sounds of *Gold Against the Soul*, then both these songs might have given you a jolt out of your leather pants. The focus was on Faster, a startling post-punk rager that based itself around its simplistic, yet sharp-edged riff. The song concerned the culture of accelerationism that the author (in this case, predominantly Edwards) seemed to believe was ripping society apart. Hard to think that this song came before the advent of the internet and the constant feedback loop of social media notifications and click-bait articles and as Bradfield would point out years later to the *NME* "There's a lot of prophecy, in terms of the acceleration of everything, joy, pain, death, consumerism."[10] Faster is indeed a prophetic song and not the Manics first or last.

What is outstanding about Faster, other than the intensity of its music, is that within this song, the band had found a perfect balance between the feelings of hopelessness that had prevailed on their earlier work and a new sense of self-belief and self-righteousness. After the voice of actor John Hurt proclaims "I want everyone corrupt" Faster properly begins with a call and response of "I am an architect/ they call me a butcher/ I am a pioneer/ they call me primitive". These lines acknowledge the criticism but discard it. As the chorus settles in with the lines "I am stronger than Mensa, Miller, and Mailer, I spat out Plath and Pinter", it is a clear declaration of the author's intellect and power over themselves. The song's best line "I know I believe in nothing, but it is my nothing" is a manifesto within the song that proclaims the author's singular vision is correct no matter the consequences.

To promote the song, the band decked themselves out in mismatched military attire and paraded upon the stage of *Top of the Pops*. As comedians Vic Reeves and Bob Mortimer introduced them to the audience the band began the performance of Faster in front of a confused looking crowd of onlookers who did their best to look like they had a smidgen of understanding of what they were witnessing. James Dean Bradfield, in military trousers and a tight army t-shirt that showed off his impressive pecs and biceps, had also decided to wear a black balaclava with the word "JAMES" scrawled crudely above the eyes. It was an interesting way to deflate the iconography of the balaclava, which had been used more obviously by IRA terrorists and of course bank robbers. Bradfield would comment to BBC Wales years later that the connection to Irish Republicanism was never the intention: "Because we were all dressed in army regalia, it felt like we were parodying the use of legitimate power, like the special forces. It didn't enter our heads that people would see it as an Irish paramilitary symbol."[11]

Single 15:

Revol (lyrics by Edwards and Wire, music by Bradfield and Moore)
Released: 1st August 1994; UK Chart Position: 22; Label: Epic; Album: *The Holy Bible*
B-sides: Too Cold Here; You Love Us (Original Heavenly Version); Love's Sweet Exile (Live); Drug Drug Druggy (Live); Roses in The Hospital (Live); You Love Us (Live) [lyrics by Edwards and Wire, music by Bradfield and Moore]
Producer: Self-Produced with Sound Engineer Alex Silva

As the band moved, jumped, stomped, and jerked along to Faster's backing track (only James' vocals were live) huge flames atop of high columns surrounded the stage. It was a health and safety officers' nightmare. It was also one of the most complained about performances in *Top of the Pops* history with over 25,000 people calling into the BBC to let their displeasure be known.

The *Top of the Pops* performance is something of Manics legend. When the band became immensely popular during 1996 onwards, these scenes and more would be played back. To the newly converted (i.e., myself) not yet schooled on the Manics history, these performances seemed out of step with the quiet and shy young men we saw now in loose khakis and polo shirts. However, as time went on and new fans became more knowledgeable, and this odd performance became more accessible via the internet, an appreciation seeped in for just how utterly against the grain the band once were.

In the run-up to the album's release, a change was noticeable. Much like the first record in which there had been an aesthetic unison, the band had decked themselves in a literal uniform of mismatched military fatigues. The band's festival performances over the summer of 1994 had a more confrontational and aggressive posture than what had been witnessed before. There was also the notable absence of Richey Edwards. Edwards had checked himself into The Priory Clinic, a rehabilitation centre for addiction and mental health. Edwards' afflictions concerned self-harm, alcoholism, and anorexia. With Edwards taking time out from the band, the other three members continued to soldier on and promote the upcoming album

The Holy Bible has been called many things: dark, depressing, difficult, apocalyptic, oppressive, nasty, the list goes on. It is all these things and more. Judging by the amount of intrigue that continues to surround the album, listeners are still, over twenty-five years later (at the time of this writing) digesting its contents. One thing that The Holy Bible is often not credited is being a good pop record. Whilst the discourse continues, I want to take this opportunity to value its accessibility as opposed to its apparent obtuseness.

<u>Album 3:</u>

The Holy Bible
Released: 30th August 1994, UK Chart Position: 6; Label: Epic
Track Listing: Yes; Ifwhiteamericatoldthetruthforonedayitsworldwouldfallapart; Of Walking Abortion; She is Suffering; Archives of Pain; Revol; 4st 7lb; Mausoleum; Faster; This is Yesterday; Die in the Summertime; The Intense Humming of Evil; P.C.P. (lyrics by Edwards and Wire, lyrics by Bradfield and Moore) Producer: Self-produced with Sound Engineer Alex Silva

---

One thing the Manics do well is write a good hummable tune that somehow wraps around their polemic style lyrics. It is a feature of their later career but also features in these early records. The Holy Bible's lyrical content should dictate that the musical accompaniment should be abrasive. But this is not always the case. Take a listen to the first track on the record, Yes. The song begins with a delicate first verse that erupts into a driving chorus. The lyrics of "In these plagued streets of pity you can buy anything" fall and rise around the guitar and make the lines "He's a boy / you wanna girl to tear off his cock" strangely joyous to sing. The next song the record Ifwhiteamericatoldthetruthforonedayit'sworldwould fallaprt (yes that really is the title and no that rogue apostrophe is not my error), despite its furious urgency, has a strange show tune element that wouldn't go amiss in a 1950s Hollywood musical. In an interview with *Loudersound*, Bradfield commented on the obtuse nature of the song: "I saw the challenge, and just how great it was – the jump from character to character, the pace of the editing was amazing. It had touches of *West Side Story*, for me."[12]

Single 16:

She is Suffering (lyrics by Edwards and Wire, music by Bradfield and Moore)
Released: 3rd October 1994; UK Chart Position: 25; label: Epic; Album: *The Holy Bible*
B-sides: Love Torn Us Under (lyrics by Edwards and Wire, music by Bradfield and Moore); The Drowners (live) [Anderson, Butler]; Stay with Me (Live) [Stewart, Wood]
Producer: Steve Brown

The record's most laughably obtuse moment comes via Revol, a song that name-checks the world's most devilish dictators and military leaders and matches them up with some kind of sexual perversion which includes "Brezhnev married into group sex" as a particular favourite of mine. Revol has an almost glam-rock stomp that pushes ahead on the song's wild lyrics. The band went ahead and released Revol as a single. As a pop song, it might have sounded like a good fit for Radio 1, but its lyrics deemed it inappropriate right from the offset.

The record's final song P.C.P fell to the wayside as the double A-side to the superior Faster, but as an album closer one could not hope for a more striking and jauntier outro.

As we move through the career of the Manic Street Preachers, we will see that the impact of *The Holy Bible* will become more apparent. In its first incarnation of release in the summer of 1994, the record was highly praised but sold poorly. The diehard fans of the band knew its importance at the time, but the general music lover was nonplussed. Only in the aftermath of the band's commercial success and mainstream popularity would *The Holy Bible* gain wider recognition among the general populace and become a constant seller.

That major success was only around the corner, but it took a devastating blow to the band for it to come.

CHAPTER THREE
The Poet Who Can't Play Guitar: The Importance of Richey Edwards

It is worth taking a short breather in the narrative of Manic Street Preachers to assess the first few years of the band's life. An extraordinary number of things, good, bad, and tragic occurred in this time frame.

On the positive side, the band released three consecutive albums that, whilst operating in the frames of rock music, were still wildly diverse and eclectic. *Generation Terrorists* had a vest of colour and spark that propelled its lyrical critique of capitalism and consumerism. *Gold Against the Soul*, whilst lyrically dour and sepia in tone, doubled down on the anthemic quality of the band's music. *The Holy Bible*, as just discussed, was morbid in its subject matter, but married this to some sharp and expressive music. Over the course of these records, the band had increased their audience share and continued a run of top forty singles. Shows across the world were packed and a devoted fan base had immersed itself in the creative world the band had made for them.

On the negative side, the band had lost their devoted manager Philip Hall to cancer towards the end of 1993.

Then came another blow, one that would continue to define them for decades. On February 1st, 1995, on the eve of a promotional tour of America alongside James Dean Bradfield, guitarist Richey Edwards checked out of London's Embassy Hotel and disappeared. To this day, his whereabouts or the circumstances of his disappearance remain shrouded in mystery. At the time, the band was not too concerned. Bradfield continued his journey to the United States to conduct radio interviews in preparation for a full band tour that was scheduled to happen later in 1995. However, when Edwards' car was discovered abandoned at a service station close to the Severn Bridge two weeks after his disappearance, the band and Edwards' family began to worry. The band went on hiatus as they processed the disappearance of their friend. As time went on, decisions about continuing as a three-piece or renaming the band were mooted.

The mystery surrounding the disappearance of Edwards has been played out in television documentaries, books, and articles. At the time of his disappearance, The Manics were not an immensely successful band, yet the story captured the attention and the imagination of the mainstream press. On any given anniversary of his disappearance or subsequent record released by the band, new sightings and riveting details are explored again to unravel what might've happened to him.

The intricacies of Richey Edwards' disappearance cannot be laid out in this short text. I recommend *Everything: A Book About Manic Street Preachers*, Simon Price's biography of the band's early days, or *A Version of Reason: The Search for Richey Edwards* by Rob Jovanovic, for an in-depth and factual analysis of what occurred. There are also several television documentaries and YouTube videos that break down the moments of disappearance. Many, however, do cross over into conspiracy theory and hearsay as sometimes the legend is far more enticing than the facts. What should always be remembered is that the disappearance of Richey Edwards was a tragic and desperate act of a troubled and greatly talented young man.

What is apparent is that Edwards' influence and intellect would continue to impact the remaining members of the band for decades to come. His presence within the world of the band would never be far away. Be it a song, or a certain lyric, or a piece of artwork, the band has continued to honour Edwards' as a continued presence in the band.

For myself, it is hard to consider Edwards in the same way older fans of the band might. I discovered the band during the arse-end of the *Everything Must Go* campaign when the band released the single Australia. Edwards was an unknown quantity to me and many others who had latched on in 1996. The band acknowledged his contributions by playing songs from *Generation Terrorists*, *Gold Against the Soul*, and on occasion *The Holy Bible* (mostly This Is Yesterday), and would include lyrics the band had been working on on *Everything Must Go*, but for journalists and TV hosts to broach the subject of his disappearance in the abundance of interviews the band were doing in 1996 was to be offered a short and sharp rebuttal from the band.

Whilst I was aware of his lyrical prowess and obvious cool aesthetics, the focus of this incarnation of the band was primarily the three core members and the amazingly uplifting music they were currently playing at this point in their career. Edwards and the first three records felt like ancient history even though when *Everything Must Go* was released in 1996, *The Holy Bible* was barely two years old.

The presence of Edwards is keenly felt and whilst he leaves the band's narrative at this point in their career, it is necessary and appropriate to acknowledge that Edwards was an incredible intellect and wry observer of society and culture. The Manics, then and today would not be the same without the affiliation with him as chief lyricist and architect of the band's style and presence.

Humour might not be an attribute associated with the Manics as a whole, and certainly not with Edwards, but read an early interview or watch a clip from one of the countless TV performances from that time in the 1990s and witness the beautiful charming wit of the lad. It was clear very early on that Edwards was destined for some kind of stardom, if that be literature, criticism, or rock and roll, and his shy, yet obvious charisma, would propel him to success in whatever path he chose.

So it is more tragic that the world didn't get more of his intellect. No doubt, Edwards would have been an excellent social critic in the age of New Labour, fully able to dissect the contradictions of Tony Blair's rule. Nicky Wire has often said that Edwards would have made an extraordinary contribution to social media, predicting to the *NME* that Edwards would have had "the biggest Twitter following in the western world – for better or for worse."[13]

Though hopefully Edwards would have used social media as a weapon to engage the culture, that sharp tongue and sarcastic tone he sometimes employed would have guaranteed a few twitter outrages along the way.

Thankfully, we have an exhaustive archive of work to look back to see that Edwards was ahead of the times in terms of his use of language and the ideas that these words conveyed. Look to Faster, for its almost prophetic notions of 24/7 informational overload. Or Natwest, Barclays, Midlands, Lloyds from *Generation Terrorists* that ruefully remarks on the "black horse apocalypse" of the banking system. He saw it all coming.

And it's not just records and lyrics that we can sit and decipher. Edwards was always keen to partake in an interview on TV or in print, any opportunity to lay out a decent soundbite. The archives of the internet are finding this stuff all the time. Shoddy VHS recordings uploaded to YouTube and translated interviews from Japanese music magazines are popping up all the time. It's a treasure trove that doesn't appear to have a bottom.

We'll leave Edwards here and continue on with the remaining three members, knowing that his influence, guidance and coolness is never far from the story.

CHAPTER FOUR
Freed from the Memory (1996-2000)

The first signs that Manic Street Preachers were back in action came on September 9th, 1995 in the form of a cover of Burt Bacharach and Hal David's standard Raindrops Keep Falling on My Head for the charity record *The Help Album*.

The record was conceived to raise funds for the War Child charity. All contributions were recorded in a single day, with acts including Oasis, Blur, Massive Attack, and Radiohead. Released during the heights of the Britpop era, the record was a huge success. The recording was a low-pressure affair for the band and signalled to the world that they were ready to resume in some fashion. Unlike the pounding and grinding of their last release *The Holy Bible,* Raindrops Keep Falling on My Head offered the listener something uniquely different from the band. A quietness and gentleness that had never really existed in the band's repertoire. Of course, the song called for it. Raindrops Keep Falling on My Head has always been a melancholic standard that since its use in the 1969 film *Butch Cassidy and the Sundance Kid* has been tied up with that feeling of deep melancholia and a strange homesickness.

And as the band braved the new reality as a three-piece it would be *Butch Cassidy and the Sundance Kid* that seemed to provide a source of comfort for the band. With forthcoming songs like Australia and the B-side Sepia directly referencing this film.

Manic Street Preachers fourth record *Everything Must Go* was a game changer for the band

and the fans that had long been immersed in the music and culture that surrounded them. With the loss of Richey Edwards as the chief lyricist and chief instigator of their aesthetics and artwork, the band intentionally scaled back the more over the top aspects of their look and sound. Gone were the feather boas and leopard print, gone were the military uniforms, gone were the stencilled slogans on their mother's blouses. The band presented a more sober version of themselves. One that would, for once, allow the music to take command.

And what music. *Everything Must Go* was filled with deep emotional and melancholic anthems that soured beyond anything the band had previously accomplished. The lyrics, for the most part written by Nicky Wire explored loss and grief, but with a sense of universal hope. Obviously, the loss was that of their friend and bandmate, but Wire used this to widen the scope to encompass something far more profound. The obvious example of this would be A Design for Life, the first single to be lifted from the record on 15 April 1996. The music presented a swirling waltz of strings and guitar that rose and fell along with the words. Wire's themes of loss are here aimed towards the British Working Class's loss of identity since Thatcher's declaration of class war and since the End of History actions that began with the fall of the Berlin Wall.

Everything Must Go

Single 17:
A Design for Life Released: 15th April 1996; UK Chart Position: 2: Label: Epic; Album: *Everything Must Go*

B-sides: Mr Carbohydrate; Dead Passive; Dead Trees and Traffic Islands; Bright Eyes (Live)
Producer: Mike Hedges, Dave Eringa

Working-class values included a good education, good manners, community spirit, and pride in one's appearance. Over a few years, this aspect of working-class pride had been eroded. This had happened on a societal level, but also a cultural one. Oasis were of course touted as working-class lads who had done good, but their antics involving drugs and alcohol and the boorish laddish manner they often presented themselves within the media betrayed their humble background. Thatcher's infamous comment that there was no such thing as society and that "There are individual men and women and there are families"[14] seemed to be Oasis's starting point. It was all about the individual success, the individual experience of rock and roll, and the ego that led the Gallagher brothers to continuously butt heads.

In Oasis's earliest single, Supersonic, the emphasis is on the "I" and the "my", the "*I* need to be *my*self", and the "Can *I* ride with you", and the "*I*'m feeling supersonic". In A Design for Life, there is no "I", only "we" and "us", "*we* only want to get drunk", "*we* are not allowed to spend", "work came and made *us* free". A Design for Life was a brilliant manifesto for breaking stereotypes and reclaiming some essence of working-class values on a more grand scale.

Of course, Oasis was probably not thinking of Thatcher as they tossed down another line of coke, but that is the point I am trying to make. The members of Manic Street Preachers were raised in a community of deep-seated working-class pride and labour unionism that was shattered by Thatcher's policies. The boys from Oasis, not so much. Thatcher was hated in the valleys. Noel Gallagher publicly aligned himself with Blair's New Labour government and has in recent years become a political centrist man denouncing both the left and right, saying that "The Tories don't care about the vulnerable, and the communists don't care about the aspirational."[15] A Design for Life sailed into the charts at number 2, the highest chart position the band had ever achieved. It was only held off the top spot by Leicester-based R'N'B sensation Mark Morrison with his hit single Return of the Mack.

The accompanying video for A Design for Life offered a bold visual interpretation of the lyrical theme. The band performed the song in a warehouse setting, whilst huge projected text ("A house is a machine for living") and visuals of the Poll Tax Riots, and Cheltenham Horse Race converge to comment on the barriers to working-class and upper-class existence.

With the song entering at number two, many of the record-buying public assumed that A Design for Life was a debut single from a new Welsh indie band. The past had receded in most people's minds and with their new clothes and sensible hairstyles, in essence, Manic Street Preachers 2.0 were, if not new, then at the very least reborn.

Of course, the song was misinterpreted. The bellowing line of "We only want to get drunk" was co-opted by the lager-swigging masses. But a good anthem, like a good democracy, should encompass everyone.

With the single a smash hit, the forthcoming album was much anticipated. Released on 20 May 1996, *Everything Must Go* was a statement of intent unlike any other. The title itself suggested that in the wake of Edwards' disappearance the past and all the baggage that went with it had to be forgotten. In the album's title song, and soon to be second single, the band pleads with the listener, and their older fans, "I just hope that you can forgive us / but everything must go". To the new listener, this might have seemed abstract, but for those with knowledge of the band's trials, it was a release and a mutual understanding for the band and the long-time fans.

<u>Album 4:</u>

Everything Must Go
Released: 20th May 1996; UK Chart Position: 2;
Label: Epic
Track Listing: Elvis Impersonator: Blackpool Pier
(lyrics by Edwards and Wire, music by Bradfield
and Moore); A Design for Life; Kevin Carter (lyrics
by Edwards); Enola/Alone; Everything Must Go;
Small Black Flowers That Grow in the Sky (lyrics
by Edwards); The Girl Who Wanted to Be God
(lyrics by Edwards and Wire, music by Bradfield
and Moore); Removables (lyrics by Edwards);
Australia; Interiors (Song for Willem de Kooning);
Further Away; No Surface All Feeling
Producer: Mike Hedges

Whilst Wire did most of the heavy-duty lifting when it came to lyrics, five songs were included that came from the pen of Edwards. The opening song, Elvis Impersonator/ Blackpool Pier set a bleak tone and the strange wash of sea waves that underpin the track makes for an uneasy listening experience. The subject of Kevin Carter concerned the life of the famous war photographer who racked with guilt over his uncompromising photos of human suffering, killed himself. The tender Small Black Flowers That Grow in The Sky matched lush acoustic guitar and plucked harp with sad imagery of caged zoo animals, a metaphor for the author's own troubles. The Girl Who Wanted to Be God was a lovely and graceful piece of orchestral pop music that concerned the tragic poet Sylvia Plath. And last but by no means least, Removables, a downtrodden acoustic strum reminiscent of Nirvana that features a frightening undercurrent of darkness that would not have gone amiss on *The Holy Bible*.

Including these Edwards penned songs on the record was a neat way to engage newer listeners with the band's past and point back to some of the darker material that lay there. In the context of the record's more joyous moments these five tracks stand-out like sore thumbs. It was credit to the band that they saw fit to release Kevin Carter as the record's third single and thus infiltrate the top ten with a song about a dead war photographer.

Single 18:

Everything Must Go
Released 22nd July 1996; UK Chart Position: 5;
Label: Epic; Album: *Everything Must Go*
B-sides: Black Garden; Hanging On; No-One Knows
What It's Like to Be Me; Raindrops Keep Fallin' on
My Head (Live) [Bacharach, David]
Producer: Mike Hedges

Everything Must Go continued to propel the band towards becoming one of the biggest-selling bands in Britain, something that only a few years ago would seem outrageous. Their welcome to the music establishment came with the nomination and subsequent win at the 1997 Brit Awards. The band was nominated in four categories, winning two for Best Group and Best Album. As the band took the stage to collect the awards from sportsmen Colin Jackson and Vinnie Jones and thank the fans for the award, Nicky Wire leaned in and shouted to the audience "This is for all the comprehensive schools that the government is trying to close. They make the best art, the best music, and the best boxers too." The band brought the heart of working-class politics to the heart of the music establishment.

<u>Single 19:</u>

Kevin Carter
Released: 30th September 1996; UK Chart Position: 9; Label: Epic; Album: *Everything Must Go*
B-sides: Horses Under Starlight; Sepia; First Republic; Everything Must Go (acoustic version)
Producer: Mike Hedges

On 2 May 1997, Tony Blair's New Labour Party was elected with a landslide victory, ending eighteen years of Tory rule. The New Labour government was a far cry from the post-war Labour government of Clement Atlee or even the 1980s opposition party under Michael Foot and Neil Kinnock. New Labour had embraced the neoliberal ethos of the Tory Party and media nemeses such as Rupert Murdoch had aligned themselves with the Blairite vision. Margaret Thatcher herself even backhandedly endorsed New Labour and took credit for the election, stating "We forced our opponents to change their minds."[16]

Of course, eighteen years of Tory rule had taken its toll on the nation and the wave of relief felt by many was hard to dismiss. For the first-time in nearly two decades, a watered-down version of the left had won the corridors of power.

On 24 May, and in the shadow of this newfound national level of optimism Manic Street Preachers would play their largest headlining show to date at Manchester's NYNEX Arena. The performance was filmed for the band's first official video release, *Everything Live*. The set list pulled predominantly from *Everything Must Go*, but also included some cuts from previous records. As was, and in some cases still is, the nature of massive arena shows, the band packed the set list with the notable hit singles and noticeably only included one song (Faster) from the difficult *The Holy Bible*.

Single 20:

Australia
Released: 2nd December 1996; UK Chart Position: 7: Label: Epic; Album: *Everything Must Go*
B-sides: Velocity Girl (James Beattie, Robert Gillespie); Take the Skinheads Bowling (Chris Molla, David Lowery, Greg Lisher, Victor Krummenacher); Can't Take My Eyes Off You (Bob Crewe, Robert Gaudio); A Design for Life (Live)
Producer: Mike Hedges

With a hit record, a collection of top ten singles, a bunch of major awards (A Design for Life would also go on to win an Ivor Novello Award and the band swept up at the *NME* awards), and a massive arena show under their belts, thoughts turned to the creation of a follow-up.

Manic Street Preachers fifth record, *This is My Truth Tell Me Yours* was arguably the first Manic Street Preachers record that the UK mainstream media, MTV, the popular radio stations, the budding internet, and the record-buying populace as a whole was actually very excited about. This is not to say that the previous records from the band had not been anticipated with great excitement. They of course had been, certainly. But the scope of those previous records had been small occasions of fanfare and appreciated by a more devoted enclave of fans. The band had never really had to consider following up on massive success before.

This was also the first Manic Street Preachers record that was solely the work of the trio of Bradfield, Wire, and Moore. Whilst the music was always a Bradfield and Moore concern *This is My Truth* was the first record to be solely authored by Wire.

In September 1998, when *This is My Truth...* was released, expectations were high. The record did not disappoint in terms of these expectations. Although Britpop was now pretty much dead in the water by this point (thanks to Oasis and their much-maligned 1997 album *Be Here Now*), the Manics had been around long before its rise and would transcend its demise with grace. As if to emphasize this, the first single to be released from the record, If You Tolerate This Your Children Will Be Next—a song that through its lyrical content addressed the real story of a group of Welsh farmers who joined the International Brigade to fight Fascism during the Spanish Civil War—landed the band their first number-one single.

Intelligence in pop music had come of age and the Manics were partly if not wholly responsible for this.

This is My Truth Tell Me Yours

Single 21:

If You Tolerate This Your Children Will Be Next
Released: 24th August 1998; UK Chart Position: 1;
Label: Epic; Album: *This is My Truth Tell Me Yours*
B-Sides: Prologue to History; Montana/Autumn 78;
Keven Carter (Live) [lyrics by Edwards]
Producer: Dave Eringa

And let just take a second to understand the scope of the album's title. *This is My Truth Tell Me Yours* was taken from a speech made by Welsh politician Aneurin Bevan, who served as Minister of Health and Housing in the post-Second World War UK government of Prime Minister Clement Atlee. Bevan was from a rough and ready working-class background, a staunch socialist, and chiefly the architect of the National Health Service and the British Welfare State. By the time *This is My Truth*'s release, the New Labour government of Tony Blair had been in power for just over a year. In this government, the socialist origins of the Labour movement had been dispensed with in favour of free-market liberalism.

The title of the record was tied up in political history yet acts as a reminder in the new dawn of political shape-shifting that there once were politicians of real integrity and real grit.

This probably was not on most listeners or possibly even the band's minds as the record debuted at number one in the album charts selling a whopping 136,000 copies in its first week. Nonetheless, it is a testament to the sheer intelligence that has always been bestowed upon a Manics record. With *This is My Truth...* gaining a footing in the European and Asian record markets, the band also embarked on a mammoth worldwide tour in support of the record.

Album 5:

This is My Truth Tell Me Yours
Released: 14th September 1998; UK Chart Position: 1; Label: Epic
Track Listing: The Everlasting; If You Tolerate This Your Children Will Be Next; You Stole the Sun from My Heart; Ready for Drowning; Tsunami; My Little Empire; I'm Not Working; You're Tender and You're Tired; Born a Girl; Be Natural; Black Dog on My Shoulder; Nobody Loved You; S.Y.M.M.
Producer: Mike Hedges, Dave Eringa

This is My Truth... as an album of two halves. The first half springs forward with emotional and melancholic anthems that had by this point become the Manics' bread and butter. It is no coincidence that four of the five opening tracks would be released as singles, and it is easy to see why. The opening songs of The Everlasting and If You Tolerate This Your Children Will Be Next were both slow-burning anthems, but the posture of these songs was sluggish in a kind of defeatism mostly reserved for old age.

The other two songs that would also become singles, You Stole the Sun from My Heart and Tsunami, though lyrically dour, bounded along and when played aloud made dancefloors and mosh pits exciting places to occupy.

The second half of the record that begins with the song My Little Empire is where the sombre tone is turned up a few notches whilst the anthemic elements are dialled right back.

It's easy to write off the second half of the record, but there is a quality to it that is not as instantaneous as those first opening moments and there are small intricacies that take time to reveal themselves over many listens. The experience is akin to the listener being allowed to pass into an interzone of extraordinary revelations and secrets. This speaks to the lyrical content, but also the musical accompaniment that drives it.

Take for example the anguished cello that lies just under My Little Empire, making the track as sombre and dark as anything on *The Holy Bible*. The next song, I'm Not Working, utilizes an incredibly dour and slow drum pattern and a distorted hum that slows the track to a funeral march. Its sonic companion is Joy Division's gloomy The Eternal. Yet where there is solemn despair there is also brightness, hope, and, dare I say, joy to be found.

Listen, for example, to the milkman whistle that suddenly bestows the already quite chipper You're Tender and You're Tired and try not to crack a smile. Or how about the gorgeous orchestral swell that sends Black Dog On My Shoulder into the hills and to new heights of emotion. Even Be Natural, a lacklustre song on first or second listen, suddenly breaks its autumnal hue and swells into an achingly beautiful and bright chorus.

The second half of *This is My Truth* also contains the starkly beautiful Born a Girl, a song that drives the listener to become an almost voyeuristic peeping Tom into the world of Nicky Wire and his desire to abandon manhood and live as a girl in body and mind.

It is interesting to take a moment to pause and reflect on Born a Girl. The title and indeed the content came at the arse end of the laddish Britpop moment in which making yourself out as feminine in any way might get you bottled. It also came just as the faux feminism of The Spice Girls was sweeping across the nation and being feminist meant taking on a brash and loud posture in the guise of "Girl Power." Born A Girl was a brave statement to make in this climate. And this does not just account for the lyrics; the music too is tender, austere, and fragile.

What makes it more effective is that whilst Wire provides the lyrical content, the song is actually sung by the very masculine form of Bradfield. The contrast in the medium and the message suddenly becomes noticeably clear. Born A Girl arrives as a crucial understanding of Manic Street Preachers as a whole. The lyrical content was always provided by Wire and Edwards and the vocal duties fell to Bradfield to communicate the ideas as a union. This had always been a successful mutual partnership. In Born a Girl, there is a sudden awareness to the listener that the Manics are individuals each contributing to the whole.

The only real misfire of *This is My Truth* is the closing song S.Y.M.M (South Yorkshire Mass Murderer), the lyrics of which broach the subject of the Hillsborough Disaster of April 1989 in which 96 people were killed in a human crush at the Hillsborough Football Stadium in Sheffield, England. Whilst the subject was close to the band's heart and they had but a year earlier played the Hillsborough Justice Concert held at Anfield Stadium, the lyrics seemed to spend a long time searching for the justification behind the writing of the song in the first place. Sonically speaking, the song is a studio created masterpiece with backward drum loops, chiming bells, haunting harmonies, and shimmering organ. Yet, it ended the record limply with no sense of accomplishment or hope.

This is My Truth... was an even bigger hit than *Everything Must Go*. The record's first single If You Tolerate This Your Children Will Be Next has become a classic standard, and the album continued the band's excellent run of top ten singles with The Everlasting, You Stole the Sun from My Heart, and Tsunami.

When the band won another round of Brit Awards in February 1999 the album hit another peak. The reaction to *This is My Truth...* from fans and critics alike was for the most part highly positive. But one thing was notable about the band's posture, they lacked energy, they lacked fire, they lacked confrontation.

All this would change during the summer of 1999. Criticism of the band's more lacklustre approach meant that come festival season the Manics were in rude form and ready to antagonize once again. The change probably drew from the rather un-rock and roll use of a private portaloo at that year's Glastonbury Festival. Leftist singer and songwriter Billy Bragg called them out on the very un-egalitarian idea of personal toilets in the week's music press and the band were rightly ridiculed for it from the other bands playing the festival to music journalists. Whilst the Glastonbury performance was a standard run through the hits and the latest record, the following month's T in The Park Festival and the V Festival saw a band back in touch with their vitriol.

Towards the end of the T in The Park appearance, the band trashed their gear and stormed off the stage. Their headlining slot at the V Festival saw Wire decked out in a lovely pink dress and knee-high socks. The band leaped around the stage like schoolboys on too much sugar. It was a wonderful change of pace to see.

As mentioned above *This is My Truth...* saw four singles released. The colossal If You Tolerate This... led the charge and was released on 24 August 1998 and went on to become the band's first number-one single. The extra tracks that accompanied the song were the other side of the coin to Tolerate epic quality. Prologue to History was an outstanding Wire lyric that dealt with the loss and influence of Richey Edwards but also name-checked Steve Ovett and Sean William Ryder. The music was a rush of jabbering keyboards, tumbling drums, and stabbed guitar. Prologue to History has the honour of being one of only a handful of B-sides that have been performed live. When the band issued the twentieth-anniversary edition of *This Is My Truth...* they switched out the last but one track, Nobody Loved You with Prologue to History. Although the song certainly deserved its place among the higher-profile songs of the mother album, it is placed (as we discussed above) in the more quiet and personal reflective part of the record seems jarring.

<u>Single 22:</u>

The Everlasting
Released: 30th November 1998, UK Chart Position: 11; Label: Epic: Album: *This is My Truth Tell Me Yours*

B-sides: Black Holes for the Young (Ft. Sophie Ellis-Bextor); Valley Boy; Small Black Flowers That Grow in the Sky (Live)
Producer: Mike Hedges

Then came The Everlasting, released on 30th November 1998, and reaching number 11, which broke their roll of top ten singles somewhat, but was still considered an excellent hit single release. The promotional video hit a snag as it featured members of the band and members of the public suddenly overcome with flames as they moved through London's Euston railway station. The release came the same week as the inquest into the death of Michael Menson, a member of the production trio Double Trouble who had been set on fire on 13 February 1997 by a group of men. The video was considered insensitive to the inquest and the digitally produced flames were removed.

One of the Manics' most interesting B-sides happens to be snuggled away on The Everlasting's CD release, the band's duet with Sophie Ellis Bexter, then of indie stalwarts theaudiance, now, of course, a highly successful solo artist. The song Blackholes for the Young addressed the London-centric aspects of society and the "cappuccinos among the fumes" enjoyed by the residents of London. It was a cheap shot of course from a band who when they very started out knew that to get anywhere in the music industry they had to move to London and play the circuit.

Single 23:

You Stole the Sun from My Heart

Released: 8 March 1999; UK Chart Position: 5;
Label: Epic; Album: *This is My Truth Tell Me Yours*
B-sides: Socialist Serenade; Train in Vain (Live)
[Strummer and Jones], If You Tolerate This Your
Children Will Be Next (Live)
Producer: Mike Hedges

The next single, You Stole the Sun from My Heart came on 8th March 1999, a few weeks after their second win for Best Band and Best Album at the previous month's Brit Awards. The single charted at number five and was accompanied by a video that saw the band performing the song whilst cute, animated birds tweeted and flew around their heads. The single included the song Socialist Serenade, which was an attack on the ethos of Tony Blair's New Labour government ("Change your name to New / Forget the fucking Labour") and a live rendition of The Clash's jaunty little rocker Train in Vain.

Single 24:

Tsunami
Released: July 5, 1999; UK Chart Position: 11;
Label: Epic; Album: *This is My Truth Tell Me Yours*
B-sides: Buildings for Dead People, A Design for
Life (Video), Motown Junk (Live) [lyrics by
Edwards and Wire, music by Bradfield and Moore]
Producer: Mike Hedges

The final single to be released off *This is My Truth...* was the song Tsunami. It was an obvious contender for a single with its electric sitar and strings that envelope the song in an air of exotic chimes. However, in typical Manics fashion, the lush instrumentation combines with the song's tragic tale of June and Jennifer Gibbons, two twin sisters who became known as "The Silent Twins". Born in Barbados, the Gibbons family moved to the U.K in the early 1960s as part of the Windrush generation of immigrants. June and Jennifer shared an almost telepathic connection that manifested itself in the pair's own private language. When they were found guilty of committing petty crimes, they were locked up for eleven years in the notorious Broadmoor Hospital. The "Tsunami" of the song was a reference to the great wave of release that June felt when Jennifer died from a mysterious heart ailment and their connection was severed.

In continuing with the excellent array of B-sides that this record provided, a song titled Buildings for Dead People saw the band explore a more fuzzed-up and murkier sound that would act as a good pointer towards their next musical endeavours.

To wind down the 20th century the band began gearing up towards their biggest ever concert. It was announced that the band would headline the massive and still relatively new Cardiff Millennium Stadium on New Year's Eve. The band had spent the 1990s climbing the rope towards superstardom and the concert was a fitting end to the decade and an excellent bookmark to place in this stage of their career.

When 31st December 1999 rolled around the event had easily sold out its capacity of 60,000 tickets. Nicky Wire remarked on how far the band had come, explaining to journalist David Owens "Ten years ago we did a gig in Cardiff to two people. Today we're playing in front of 60,000 people. I think that shows how far we've come, how far we have grown, and how much Wales has grown."[17]

The concert proceeded without a hitch and featured a set list pulling from all corners of the band's career. For the new fans, there were the biggest and most recent hits, for the hardcore, Motown Junk from the Heavenly era and the Of Walking Abortion from *The Holy Bible*. The band did not shy away from their political origins. Before the band played their biggest hit, If You Tolerate This Your Children Will Be Next, Arthur Scargill, the Welsh Union leader who went head-to-head with Thatcher during the Miners' Strike of the 1980s broadcast a New Year's message to those gathered. And just as the band launched into their last song of the evening, the immortal A Design for Life, the cameras filming the show (the performance would be edited and released as the film *Leaving the 20th Century*) switched to live broadcast and two billion people who were watching the many events from across the globe were suddenly faced with a very sweaty and pumped up Welsh rock band singing about the virtues of a working-class existence. The Situationists could not have dreamt up anything better.

Single 25:

Masses Against the Classes
Released: 10th January 2000; UK Chart Position: 1; Label: Epic; Album: Non-album single
B-sides: Close My Eyes; Rock and Roll Music (Berry)
Producer: Dave Eringa

As a final salute to the 20th Century, the band issued a one-off single, Masses Against the Classes, a punkier standard than anything on *This is My Truth* and one that reflected on the band's previous bad blood with the music press and featured a Noam Chomsky quote and rang out with an Albert Camus quotation. It felt like the band was rediscovering their fire. But whilst Masses Against the Classes marked the final word in the band's decade, it also made a surprise citation to the beginning of the new century. The single entered the charts at number one becoming the first number-one single of the new millennium.

CHAPTER FIVE
The Paralysed Future (2001-2007)

It would be another thirteen months before the world heard what Manic Street Preachers had been cooking up. And unlike the usual first single to signal a forthcoming album, the Manics released two to showcase that the new record was a diverse musical adventure and that the band was taking risks once again.

The singles, So Why So Sad and Found That Soul were both released on 26th February 2001. Always one to look out for their fan's pockets, the singles could be purchased together for a fiver. So Why So Sad charted at number nine and Found That Soul one place higher at number 8. Only 200 copies separated the two singles.

Single 26:

So Why So Sad
Released: 26th February 2001; UK Chart Position: 8; Label: Epic; Album: *Know Your Enemy*
B-sides: Pedestal; You Stole the Sun from My Heart (Live)
Producer: Dave Eringa

Single 27:

Found That Soul
Released: 26th February 2001; UK Chart Position: 9; Label: Epic; Album: *Know Your Enemy*

B-sides: Locust Valley; Ballad of the Bangkok
Novotel; Masses Against the Classes (Live)
Producer: Dave Eringa

So Why So Sad was perhaps the most
different of the two songs and showed a side to the
band that had been rarely seen. The song is full of
sunny and joyous Beach Boys-style harmonies and
sleigh bells that betray its quite dour lyrical subject
matter. The song was paired up with a sunny and
bright promotional video that featured the band
playing the song inside a lavish studio apartment that
overlooked an idyllic beach. Things turn sour when
the families and beach bums enjoying the sunshine
are suddenly invaded by a heavily armed militia.
Although the invasion goes unnoticed by the sun-
kissed revellers and even the band themselves as
bombs explode and troops parachute into the chaos.

At the time of the song's release, the world
was still in a relatively peaceful moment. Although
the events of September 11th, 2001 would be long
remembered as the trigger point to war and unrest
that still inflict our societies today. The implication
from the So Why So Sad music video is that we as a
culture had become numb to war and conflict and no
longer allowed the travesty to occupy our time. We
continued to go on holiday, buy fancy cars, nice
clothes, anything to block out the misery of other
peoples and other countries' conflicts. It was quite a
powerful and political statement and if made post-
9/11 or when Britain and the United States teamed
up as allies for the war in Afghanistan and Iraq would
have seen the Manics potentially blacklisted for being
unpatriotic to the cause.

The flip side of So Why So Sad was Found That Soul. The song offered a blast of pure energy and acted as a manifesto for the forthcoming record. Fusing punk guitars and hammering organs the song starts strong and never relents for a moment. One could, after hearing a defeated and subdued sounding Manics on *This is My Truth Tell Me Yours*, breathe a sigh of relief that the band was once again utilizing the volume dial on their amps.

Album 6:

Know Your Enemy
Released: 19th March 2001; UK Chart Position: 2; Label: Epic
Track Listing: Found That Soul; Ocean Spray (lyrics by Bradfield); Intravenous Agnostic; So Why So Sad; Let Robeson Sing; The Year of Purification; Wattsville Blues; Miss Europa Disco Dancer; Dead Martyrs; His Last Painting; My Guernica; The Convalescent; Royal Correspondent; Epicentre; Baby Elián; Freedom of Speech Won't Feed My Children
Producers: Dave Eringa, Greg Haver, David Holmes, Mike Hedges

---

And this is where *Know Your Enemy* comes into play. This album is the eccentric and untameable child of Manic Street Preachers' records. Yet it conveys all the musical and lyrical directions that can be found in the Manics back catalogue into one (almost) digestible form. One could even argue that a song like The Convalescent, which comes at just after the halfway point in the record, packs more pop culture figures and references into a few minutes than the entire Manics back catalogue combined. What song has the gall to place golfer Payne Stewart and shock-rocker Marilyn Manson (included here as Brian Warner) alongside artist Pablo Picasso and filmmaker Werner Herzog?

When the band came out promoting *Know Your Enemy* in the various music magazines, they talked it up as the most extreme and rabble-rousing record of their career. This would have been a fair assessment if only they had stuck by it. Yet when asked by *Noisey* to rank his own records a few years later, James Dean Bradfield put it second from the bottom (above 2004's *Lifeblood*) as the least favourite. It often appears hovering in the final numbers of most fan-made lists as well, although the years have proven to be kind and it jumps up in these listings every now and again.

But why? You'll be familiar from this book's introduction that *Know Your Enemy* occupies my own thoughts quite a lot. It's a record I find utterly fascinating and equally frustrating.

The reasons for the negative consensus towards *Know Your Enemy* are varied, but to take a quick glance, the musical styles of the record are wildly diverse yet also incoherent with no real past pointers, no set pattern or path to guide the listener through. We get straight-up punk rock with songs like Dead Martyrs and Intravenous Agnostic, melancholic anthems like Let Robeson Sing, breezy west coast rock signified by So Why So Sad and Year of Purification, and of course a disco song in the shape of Miss Europa Disco Dancer, plus some slumbering blues in the aptly titled Wattsville Blues.

The politics of *Know Your Enemy* is also messy, the band seemed to want to revive the vibrant mood and social/cultural commentary of *Generation*

Terrorists and *The Holy Bible*, but the idealism of youth was absent.

The band launched the record in the communist hotbed of Havana, Cuba, dangerously flirting with the Castro regime and bloody revolutions. It was a bold move, yet also one they took a lot of heat for in the British press, especially as documentaries and photos emerged of the band shaking hands with Fidel Castro.

This leads to another point. Bradfield, Wire, and Moore were indeed older; their reintegrated political idealism came across as stubborn and grouchy in interviews from around this record's release. Yet, despite all of this, *Know Your Enemy* holds more relevance and significance than fans, and even the band themselves would give it credit for. The record remains a brilliant and defiant statement against the boring and apolitical atmosphere of music and culture at this point in time.

Single 28:

Ocean Spray (lyrics by Bradfield)
Released: 4th June 2001; UK Chart Position: 15;
Label: Epic; Album: *Know Your Enemy*
B-sides: Groundhog Days, Just A Kid, Little Trolls
Producer: Dave Eringa

Another point to make is that the record is also as raw as the Manic Street Preachers had been in a long while. Not since their earliest Blackwood demos of the late 1980s, those same demos we touched upon earlier, or the scratchy bombast of the Heavenly recordings of Motown Junk and You Love

Us, had we had such a potent, instinctive and unrefined version of the band.

After the polished sheen of *Gold Against the Soul*, *Everything Must Go* and *This is My Truth*… it was shocking, yet also exhilarating to hear the band impose a new set of rules upon themselves and endeavour to accomplish something entirely different from the past. There is spontaneity and rawness to the recordings of Intravenous Agnostic and My Guernica for example that signify the loose nature of the band's instinctive approach to making *Know Your Enemy*.

Know Your Enemy is a critical album because it acts as a pivotal point to previous incarnations of the band and as an indicator of what their future as a band might hold. *Know Your Enemy* is a requirement. It needed to be made, it needed to reference the past, yet also set the future in motion. Without its failures, the reinvention and ambition we see on future records like *Send Away the Tigers Journal for Plague Lovers*, and *Futurology* might not have even existed. Hell, the band themselves might not have existed.

Whilst some tracks on the record do not fall into what might be considered a "classic Manics" category of jump-along anthems like Faster, Motorcycle Emptiness, Australia or Design For Life, the record remains a genuine attempt by the band to explore new avenues in sound, embrace their base political views, reinvent themselves away from the shadow of Richey Edwards, renew their stance as music industry provocateurs, antagonize other bands, and basically be the band many fans, old and new, really wanted them to be at this point in their career.

Therefore, *Know Your Enemy* appears to be highly important.

But there are other more personal reasons as well. I, along with many other new fans of the band, simply were not around first-hand to witness albums like *Generation Terrorists* or *The Holy Bible*, but we were there when those first singles from *Know Your Enemy* were played on the radio and when the record itself was released. Memories of walking into HMV on the day of release, purchasing a copy, and then impatiently riding the bus home with the record in hand are crystal clear. So are my memories of arriving home, skipping dinner and heading straight to my bedroom and slipping the CD in the player and hearing those bursting chords of Found That Soul erupt from the speakers. This was no typical Manic Street Preachers record.

Yes, there were severe disappointments and misfires in songs like Miss Europa Disco Dancer, and Wattsville Blues, but there were also some amazing surprises like the Bradfield composition Ocean Spray, the gentle Baby Elian, and the brutal fuzz of My Guernica. Eventually, the disappointments morphed into grim fascinations.

There are certainly positive and negative experiences of *Know Your Enemy*, yet The sheer audacity of the album is much to be admired. If there was ever a record that explained our own current political and cultural mishaps (no matter where you live right now) then *Know Your Enemy* might just be it.

It was somewhat a shame then that with all the diversity on offer, and heavier tracks to promote the record, the Manics chose a selection of softer sounding singles that did not really reflect the aggressive nature of *Know Your Enemy*.

On 4th June 2001, the band issued the album's second track Ocean Spray as a single. The lyrics were solely written by Bradfield and dealt with the death of his mother, Sue. The Ocean Spray of the song was the literal cranberry drink that whilst sick Sue quaffed back in litres to fight off infection. The musical accompaniment is mostly an acoustic strum that after the chorus breaks into a heavy electric guitar. The song also features a rare Sean Moore trumpet solo and begins with a spoken word introduction by Manics photographer Mitch Ikeda in his native Japanese tongue. The song reached number 15 in the UK Official Singles Charts and whilst the band recorded a live performance of the song for *Top of the Pops*, the recording was not aired, possibly due to the lower than expected chart position. The song was backed with the remarkable B-sides Groundhog Days, which featured a Nicky Wire spoken word rant, and the delightful Just a Kid, whilst the cassette format of the single (sadly the last the band would issue) featured the angry Little Trolls.

Single 29:

Let Robeson Sing
Released: 10th September 2001; UK Chart Position: 19; Label: Epic; Album: *Know Your Enemy*
B-sides: Masking Tape; Didn't My Lord Deliver Daniel; Let Robeson Sing (Video); Let Robeson Sing (Live); Fear of Motion
Producers: Dave Eringa, Mike Hedges

The final single to be released from *Know Your Enemy* was the beautiful and anthemic Let Robeson Sing. The song remains an important moment for understanding the greatness of Manic Street Preachers music. As we've mentioned before, they have always had a tendency to pull focus on one real or fictionalized member of the pop culture fraternity, and here the band creates a memorable dedication to this icon of twentieth-century life.

Paul Robeson was a black American actor, singer, and civil rights activist. He became involved in political activism with the outbreak of the Spanish Civil War (1937–1939) and gave moral support to the leftist Republican troops and the International Brigade fighting against Franco's Falange. In the era of McCarthyism, the paranoia of leftist politics reached fever pitch, and Robeson, along with many other artists, writers, actors, and singers was blacklisted.

Whilst Let Robeson Sing might be the life of the album, it could also be an indicator of its death. Released as a single the day before the September 11, 2001, terrorist attacks, the song's anti-Americanism was certainly at odds with the defiant spirit that the US and its allies around the world were taking as the causes and consequences of the attack unfolded over the days, weeks and months after.

For a start, the song was critical of the anti-Communist McCarthy era, but more importantly the fabric of the American Dream itself, "the lie of the USA" as it was called, and critical of US Foreign Policy, which in the subsequent months after the attack was being pumped up with jingoistic flare. It might seem odd that the very Welsh Manic Street Preachers would openly sing about a disgraced actor from mid-twentieth-century America, but Robeson deserved his reappraisal, and like so many forgotten, or under-appreciated icons, the Manics saw triumph and failure as equally important.

The single was backed up with the B-sides Masking Tape, a cover of Robeson's traditional standard Didn't My Lord Deliver Daniel, and the quiet and breezy sounding Fear of Motion. CD2 of the release also featured a remix by Felix da Housecat and, in this author's opinion one of the most stranger remixes of a Manics song by Stone Roses frontman Ian Brown, that maintained the emotional highs of the original but featured a curious midsection rap by Brown.

As I have previously explained, *Know Your Enemy*, to my mind, is an especially important and vital record, one that reflects on the past and involves the future. Its diversity is maybe its downfall. The record sold well, but not in the same vein as *Everything Must Go* or *This is My Truth*... and it certainly did not provide the hit singles and sell-out tours that sustain a rock band.

The Manics needed to provide the audience with some crowd-pleasing releases and so on 28 October 2002, in perfect time for those early Christmastime shoppers, the band compiled and released a 'Best of' collection.

Titled *Forever Delayed*, the collection contained eighteen of the band's best-known singles and two newly recorded songs, Door to The River and There by The Grace of God. The album offered a nonlinear historical retelling of the band's recorded output, mixing recent hits from the mega-selling albums *Everything Must Go* and *This is My Truth*... with older singles.

The nonlinear approach meant that songs like the graceful The Everlasting rubbed up against the snarky Motown Junk. It made for a destabilizing listening experience, but encapsulated the band's diversity nonetheless.

Single 30:

There by The Grace of God
Released: 14th October 2002; UK Chart Position: 6;
Label: Epic; Album: *Forever Delayed*
B-sides: Automatik Teknicolour; It's All Gone;
Unstoppable Salvation; Happy Ending
Producers: Mike Hedges, Greg Haver

To promote the collection, the band issued There by The Grace of God as a single and left the elegant beauty of Door to The River to simmer as an album track.

Yet the retrospective mood did not stop there. On 14 July 2003, the Manics issued a two-disc B-side and rarities collection titled *Lipstick Traces: A Secret History of Manic Street Preachers* that pulled songs and cover versions from all parts of their career. Disc one of the collection featured twenty of the band's B-sides that, like *Forever Delayed*, were listed in a nonlinear order. Disc two of the collection featured live and recorded cover versions that had appeared as B-sides, hidden tracks, or as was the case with the blinding rendition of Nirvana's Been a Son, recorded especially for the collection.

In this case, it did not really matter how the collection was ordered. This release was to reward the diehard fans of the band who had longed for a solid collection of this material for ages. But even newer fans had longed to hear some of the songs included within the collection. Since the Manics got massive from 1996 onwards, the band's previous single releases had become much sought after. Coming across a fairly priced 12-inch single in the stacks of record fair or a charity shop was like hitting the jackpot. Record stores across the country knew what they had and saw the demand rise, and put the prices up accordingly. Thus, newer fans wanting to start their collection and hear these B-sides and cover versions were often priced out. When *Lipstick Traces* hit the shops in 2003, even I had not managed to hear all the songs included. YouTube, Spotify, and Apple Music have made it far easier to track down rare recordings and even B-sides themselves have become redundant in the age of online music streaming. Even the Manics seemed to have abandoned the practice of including B-sides. From the six singles released from 2018's *Resistance is Futile*, only one featured a new song to accompany the main track. The rest were released alone or with a remix version.

Of course, *Lipstick Traces* could not please everyone. Tracks such as Patrick Bateman (B-side to From Despair to Where), Dead Yankee Drawl (Little Baby Nothing), and Too Cold Here (Revol) were blinding omissions in most fans' opinions.

Retrospection is sometimes a good thing for a band to do. An opportunity to clear the deck and start afresh. After the critical unease towards *Know Your Enemy*, releasing two compilations in the aftermath was maybe a wise career choice.

But Manic Street Preachers have hardly been good at consistency. On 18th October 2004 the band issued their weirdest single, The Love of Richard Nixon, a bouncy electronica led song that might not have been pro-Nixon as such, but still was controversial in appraising the former United States President. The song was a signal for the forthcoming album, titled *Lifeblood*.

The Love of Richard Nixon
Released: 18th October 2004; UK Chart Position: 2;
Label: Epic; Album: *Lifeblood*
B-sides: Everyone Knows/Nobody Cares;
Everything Will Be; Askew Road, *Quarantine (In My Place of)* (short film); Voodoo Polaroids
Producers: Greg Haver, Tom Elmhirst

The members of Manic Street Preachers, especially singer and guitarist Bradfield have been rather unkind to the band's seventh album. Bradfield has described it as a product of a period in which the band had simply run out of juice and that the results were "disconnected" and "quite blood-less." The whole venture is dismissed by Bradfield in the 2015 documentary *No Manifesto* as "a strange anomaly" in the band's saga.

From the perspective of observing the band as a vital, vitriolic, and colourful punk rock hot-mess, *Lifeblood* is certainly a standout since it does not venture into the band's previous audio territory.

Lifeblood's sound and scope is cold, airy, whiteness, treated guitar sounds, programmed beats, and icy synths. Sonically speaking, it veers quite a distance from previous records and in hindsight, subsequent ones too. The record is jarring for all the wrong reasons: easing the listener in, soothing the soul, a record you might stick on during a dinner with (very left-leaning) friends, or a comedown after a heavy weekend binge. Descriptions that are wildly absent in association with the band's ethos.

But is this a bad thing? Occasionally are, we, the listeners, not allowed to simply enjoy and let the music wash over us without the added baggage?

Of course we are. The Manics had hardly ever given us an inch.

<u>Album 7:</u>

Lifeblood
Released: 1st November 2004, UK Chart Position: 13; Label: Sony
Track Listing: 1985; The Love of Richard Nixon; Empty Souls; A Song for Departure; I Live to Fall Asleep; To Repel Ghosts; Emily; Glasnost; Always/Never; Solitude Sometimes Is; Fragments (lyrics by Wire and P. Jones); Cardiff Afterlife
Producers: Tony Visconti, Tom Elmhirst, Greg Haver

I recall excitedly purchasing the record on its day of release wondering to myself what delights could be included. *Know Your Enemy* had been a scatter-brained riot of genre and colour. Their trip to Cuba to launch the record felt like forging a new direction in punk rock internationalism. So, *Lifeblood*, I thought, would surely be an extension of this.

Upon opening the CD, an advertisement for a forthcoming 10th-anniversary edition of the band's third record *The Holy Bible* fell out, an exciting reminder of the band's radical past in which they thought songs about various 20th-century dictators (I'm talking Revol here) could be a hit single. Of course, the first single from *Lifeblood* concerned disgraced U.S president Richard Nixon, so the political content of the past was still apparent here.

But the small advert of *The Holy Bible* held a somewhat stark comparison to the music and style of *Lifeblood*. Whereas on *The Holy Bible*—and to an extent, any Manic Street Preachers record you care to mention—the lyrics are crammed and distorted in order to include them in a song format, *Lifeblood* gives space and air to drift in between the compositions—an alarming and disorientating feature.

There are not many sonic predecessors in the Manic Street Preachers' back catalogue to prepare for this departure in sound. *This is My Truth Tell Me Yours* included audio experimentation with sound and space on songs such as I'm Not Working and S.Y.M.M. A number of remixes included on B-sides might slow or compress the original song into something lighter and airier. The band's collaboration with 808 State on the 1997 song Lopez offers an indicator that they had "slow and chill" in their musical arsenal, whilst the tracks Door to The River and There by The Grace of God, included on the hits collection *Forever Delayed*, experimented in sparsity and synths, ultimately remained distinctively Manics.

Yet, whilst *Lifeblood* has had its fair share of disses from the band, the record has only grown in appreciation from the fans' perspective. At first, it was discounted as a trip-up along with *Know Your Enemy*, but it has gained as the band's fortunes turned around in the post-*Send Away the Tigers* era of 2007.

My initial reaction to *Lifeblood*'s sparse and cold nature meant that my original thinking was that it was a record with little of the band's bread-and-butter political polemics. It felt and sounded like a record with nothing to say, which, in the times in which it was released, felt like a requirement of any artistic statement. Green Day, for example, had released *American Idiot* (2004) only a few weeks prior, and whilst that band had adopted the anarchism of punk rock aesthetics, social and political commentary were not what they were necessarily known for. A political band like Manic Street Preachers could have written the record of anti-establishment, anti-corporatism, anti-war, anti-Bush and Blair treatise in their sleep. They apparently chose not to and with that decision came my initial disappointment.

In some respects, this belief was wrongheaded. Despite being delivered in an autumnal tone, the lyrical content of *Lifeblood* is actually still apparent.

Take for example the very first single released from *Lifeblood*. A highly danceable bop that featured a music video with the band donning Nixon masks and playing badminton, The Love of Richard Nixon is weird and fun, but also slightly misguided in its lyricism. There was very little need to justify a Republican President who was deemed a crook when in 2004 the U.S. President at the time, George W. Bush was accused of stealing the 1998 Presidential election from Democrat Al Gore and implementing a regime of patriotic jingoism and instigating a War on Terror, which was more about rooting out insurgency at home than abroad.

The song defends the legacy of one of the United States' most divisive and crooked public figures by calling attention to the former President's diplomatic work in China and his signing of the National Cancer Act of 1971, the President's supposed "War on Cancer." I suppose this acts as a backhanded compliment and a knowing wink to the listener that really the band is being sarcastic. Political journalist Chris Hedges referred to Richard Nixon in his speech Death of the Liberal Class, as the "last truly liberal president...because he was actually afraid of liberal movements; civil liberties, labour, the environment,"[18]

The line from the song "cowering behind divided curtains" summarizes the paranoia of the Nixon administration, and Hedges examples this also by describing a scene accounted to Henry Kissinger in which Kissinger and Nixon are "cowering" in the Oval Office, watching as the Vietnam War protestors crash through a line of parked school buses defending the White House.[19]

An argument that has been made countless times about Manic Street Preachers is that the lyrics, artwork, and whole aesthetics of the band lead the listener down various trails of discovery. In my own time as a fan of the band, I've read up on the Spanish Civil War, the singer and activist Paul Robeson, feminist writer and author of *S.C.U.M. Manifesto* Valerie Solanas, and Fidel Castro and the Cuban Revolution, all because they featured in a song or a quote was placed on the artwork of a single release. Perhaps The Love of Richard Nixon is *Lifeblood*'s only true political song, but there is still content that draws the listener to want to learn more.

The graceful Emily concerns Emily Pankhurst, a political activist, and a leader in the British women's suffrage movement. Whilst the title of Glasnost and To Repel Ghosts (but not the song's content) leads the listener to the dying embers of the Soviet Union, the end of the Cold War and the End of History as a whole and the paintings and life of Jean-Michel Basquiat respectively.

In and around these songs are more subtle and personal reflections. The opening song 1985 looks back on the author's formative years of reading, writing, and engaging with the popular culture of the time. It is a subject that returns again and again in the themes of Manic Street Preachers songs, most successful and most warmly in 2013's Rewind the Film and *The Holy Bible*'s This Is Yesterday. But here, with the atmosphere and artic chill of the composition, the picture painted is oppressively melancholic.

The closing track Cardiff Afterlife refers to the band's missing guitarist and lyricist Richey Edwards and the permanent knowledge of not knowing his whereabouts or the circumstances of his disappearance. The track refers to this state as the "paralyzed future" of the band, and indeed the presence of Edwards is not something the band have been able to shake off easily.

In hindsight, the Manics have not made much effort in distancing themselves from their own history. The numerous reissues of past records and reminders of Edwards in lyrical content are obvious signifiers. Cardiff Afterlife, as much as it is about Edwards, is also a song that deals with the band's fragmenting relationship. After *Lifeblood*'s lukewarm assessment from fans and critics, the band would take several years off, and Bradfield and Wire would in the interim release solo albums that might have indicated a severed alliance. Thankfully, this did not happen and, as we'll soon discover, the pause in the band's narrative allowed for renewed vigour.

There is a sense that *Lifeblood* is apolitical and reflective for a particularly good reason. The horrors of the world at this time were so apparent that an attempt to make an articulate comment on the mess would have been daunting. The Manics have always signposted authoritarianism and abuses of power, but not always during times of apparent overreach of authority. For example, If You Tolerate This Your Children Will Be Next, the band's ode to those that took up arms against Fascism during the Spanish Civil War came out in late 1998, more than one year into Tony Blair's New Labour Government, a time in the country's history of prosperity and renewed national vitality. Blair was not the pariah he would become in his second and third term, but a modern, hip, and good-looking leader who played guitar and hung out with Oasis. Fascism was a thing of history, so the song surely wasn't a warning worth hearing? The ideology was gone, dead and buried for certain. Right?

Or how about performing the 2010 single Some Kind of Nothingness on Britain's most popular television show, *Strictly Come Dancing*, whilst the student protests of November and December 2010 engulfed the country. One of the biggest uprisings in recent times were directed at the Conservatives and the Liberal Democrats coalition government's decision to increase student fees, despite campaign promises from the Lib Dems to abolish these fees completely. Thousands protested, whilst the Manics, decked out in suits and ties, plugged a mediocre single to millions of viewers.

Or what about the band's most recent, at least at the time of writing, album *Resistance Is Futile*. The only songs that really challenged the climate of fake news, Trumpian lies, and Brexit chaos was Distant Colours and The Left Behind. The rest of the record, as bassist Nicky Wire remarked, was an opportunity to look at "art" as "a hiding place."[20] Thus, songs on Yves Klein, David Bowie, Vivian Maier, and Dylan

Thomas provided great portals for listeners to fall down but did not provide much commentary on the state of the world.

Before I am called out here for dismissing the Manics' politics, this pattern of expressing political convictions at non-political times in history and vice versa, should actually be applauded. The Manics have continually reminded us of our complacency in decent times and have given us a "hiding place" in times of trouble. Right now, our world is collapsing into chaos and the themes of If You Tolerate This… are suddenly apparent in the rise of neo-Nazism and hard-right terrorism across the globe. Thank god we have them.

Single 33:

Empty Souls
Released: 10th January 2005; UK Chart Position: 2; Label: Epic; Album: *Lifeblood*
B-sides: All Alone Here; No Jubilees; Litany; Dying Breeds (Video); Failure Bound
Producer: Greg Haver

The Manics have a catalogue of records that act as primers for the times, but also places to hide when required. That is what *Lifeblood* provided at the time and what it continues to provide today. It remains a truly delicate exercise and rare reflective episode in the Manics' career to date. But it also feels like an abandoned promise. The only other single released from the record was the quite beautiful and autumnal Empty Souls. This charted at a very respectable number 2 in the UK single charts. Despite the success of the single, it already appeared like the band were moving on and were resigned to the fact that *Lifeblood* had been drained of its potential.

Never a band to concede, Manic Street Preachers set out on a retrospective tour, Past, Present, Future, during the Spring of 2005, which allowed them some immense freedom to perform rarely played songs and visit venues in towns and cities they hadn't visited in years. One performance at Southampton Guildhall kicked off with a savage performance of *The Holy Bible*'s Of Walking Abortion.

Extended Play 3:

God Save the Manics
Released: 19 April 2005; UK Chart Position: n/a
(free download/promo limited to 3000 copies);
Label: Sony Music
Track listing: A Secret Society; Firefight;
Picturesque
Producer: Dave Eringa

To commemorate the tour, the band issued a limited-edition EP titled God Save the Manics on April 20, 2005. The EP featured three tracks that might have been destined for the abandoned third *Lifeblood* single. As a set of songs there is some interest and pointers to what was to come. The song Firefight, for example, is the second release to which the lyrics were solely written by Bradfield. As we will discuss shortly, Bradfield was prepping for his own solo release. Unknown at the time of the EP's release, the track, Picturesque was a composite of lyrics handed over to the band by Richey Edwards not long before his disappearance in 1995. These lyrics would materialise later on the band's ninth album *Journal for Plague Lovers* in 2009 as the songs All Is Vanity and Doors Closing Slowly.

After the lacklustre response to *Lifeblood*, Manic Street Preachers opted for a short hiatus. It was not long before the creative itch was felt and both Bradfield and Wire announced solo records. Both came out within two months of each other in 2006. Bradfield's *The Great Western* landed first on July 24th and Wire's *I Killed the Zeitgeist* on September 25th. Whilst both records have merit, it is worth considering them as a package to better understand the nature of their relationship to the mother band.

The Great Western is a glorious soul guitar record which allows Bradfield as a vocalist room to breathe and his lyrics flow out. The only track that shares any similarity to the Manic Street Preachers core sound is the opening track and first single That's No Way to Tell a Lie with its stabbing guitar lines and shouty vocals. After this, the record falls into a steady flow of ballads and anthemic rock songs.

Nicky Wire's solo record *I Killed the Zeitgeist* was something of a revelation. It was musically capable, with stomping indie and surging punk rock, as well as some touching ballads. The record was also lyrically superb, touching on personal angst, loss, and hope. In the past, Wire had been viewed as a competent bass player but a terrible singer. His vocal turn on Wattsville Blues from *Know Your Enemy* was unapologetically out of tune and dreary. Lou Reed meets Mark E. Smith on a binge of cigarettes and a bout of flu was the positive way to describe it. Yet *I Killed the Zeitgeist* disproved this. When the music matched Wire's voice, his singing became an impressive counterpart, and the lyrics took on an even more desperate means of communication in

Wire's drawl and drone. It also showed that Wire as a musician had been overlooked somewhat. Yet this should not have been the case at all. His bass work on *The Holy Bible* had given that record a sense of guidance and underlying doom and gloom that perfectly captured the mood of the record. His bass lines are the record's bleeding broken heart. Look also to *Everything Must Go*, especially on the track Interiors (Song for Willem DeKooning) in which the bass lines fight and throb against the verse before letting go and exploding into one of the record's best and most progressive choruses.

What is fascinating is that despite the two records' obvious differences in sound and style, they form two sides of the same coin and perfectly encapsulate the influences and contradictions of the Manic Street Preachers.

CHAPTER SIX
A Review of *No Manifesto*

We are, give or take a month or two at the halfway point in the narrative of Manic Street Preachers' career. The first half was full of extreme lows and giddy highs, of music that pierced almost unbearable darkness yet moved to exquisite light and power. It was fitting that at this point in their career a documentary film was in the works. Although it would not see the light of day until 2015, the film, titled *No Manifesto* lands smack bang in the centre of the era in which we currently find ourselves. The below text was originally published as a review in *The Quietus* on March 13, 2015. Apart from a few tidy-ups here and there the text is as it was published.

I recall a conversation myself and a fellow Manic Street Preachers aficionado had when *No Manifesto* was first announced sometime in 2006/7. Firstly, both of us were particularly peeved at the title of the film. Being uppity Manics fans we stated in our know-all capacity that the Manics had laid out a very clear manifesto at their very origins: famously proposing that their debut album *Generation Terrorists* was the only one they would ever need to record, that it was sell sixteen million copies and lead to a sell-out show at Wembley Stadium. The band would then break up and disappear leaving the adoring masses weeping in the streets at the loss of rock and roll's saviours and destructors.

      Of course, like most manifestos, it failed to transpire. The public were not ready to take a bunch of Welsh, lipstick and leopard print wearing, slogan spouting, punk rock pretty boys to their collective hearts.

Our second grievance (or at the very least my own) was that the filmmaker, Elizabeth Marcus, had begun production during a lull period in the band's history. What good was a vigorous rock documentary when the band in question had just released the mostly lifeless album *Lifeblood*? The band were also in the midst of a career retrospective, with the greatest hits collection *Forever Delayed*, a B-sides and rarities compilation *Lipstick Traces*, and a ten-year anniversary edition of their monolithic album *The Holy Bible*. All this nostalgic activity made it obvious how plodding and uninspired some of *Lifeblood* really was (the album is dismissed in *No Manifesto* in less than a minute, with James Dean Bradfield calling it a "strange anomaly").

Archive footage of the band's heyday in army fatigues and balaclavas, screaming out the nihilistic anthem Faster on *Top of the Pops* would surely now show the band in a state of decline; musically, physically, and aesthetically. The military attire would be replaced by loose khakis and designer brand shirts. The following years offered solo offerings, but little band activity. Lead singer and guitarist James Dean Bradfield's solo debut *The Great Western* was well received and had genuine moments of greatness, whilst bassist Nicky Wire's *I Killed the Zeitgeist*, was a shabby punk-pop oddity. Although unbeknownst to fans and critics at the time, the Manics were building towards a triumphant critical and commercial rebirth that would begin with the release of *Send Away the Tigers* (2007). However, as it stood here, *No Manifesto* was doomed to failure, and therefore to be denounced.

After viewing the film, I wish I could go back in time and give my self-righteous self a good kicking. Elizabeth Marcus has produced a cracking, if slightly uneven, fan film. It may not measure up to classic rock documentaries of the past, but it blows apart the pretensions of previous television documentaries on the subject of the band, which have tended to be sober reflections on their still missing guitarist, lyricist, and friend Richey Edwards. Though I would still argue that, despite the film's title, the Manic Street Preachers have intuitively produced a solid career long manifesto with the aim of shining a light on various cultural figures, historical events, political dramas, and personal traumas. There are not many bands who can claim that promoting intellectualism for a mainstream audience is a vital part of their existence. This facet of fierce intelligence has continued throughout their career. As the years rolled on the meanings may have become more refined, but they were still there, nestled within the music and ready to illuminate the audience.

In *No Manifesto* the band mostly talk about their career, and muso stuff like guitar collections and drum kits. It is fascinating to watch the band in the unglamorous surroundings of a Cardiff rehearsal studio, and it is obvious that they savour the environment of creativity. Their fans, culled from various nationalities, cutely comment on James, Nicky, and Sean as individuals, as if they were proud aunts and uncles to three overachieving nephews. They construct the band's history and debunk some Manic myths (Nicky Wire can actually play the bass really well!). The interviews also include some of the band's entourage; a roadie and a couple of their producers, but unfortunately the documentary fails to take in some of the bands more interesting associates. It would have been good to have author and columnist John Niven, actor Michael Shannon, the band's official photographer Mitch Ikeda, biographer Simon Price, or music photographer Kevin Cummins, all confirmed Manics fans, lend some weight to the discussion of the band's impact. Marcus does consult an extremely small number of American Manics fans, which at the very least brings to light an obscure subculture of devotion to the band that has mostly gone unreported.

Focusing on a lacklustre period was an early criticism. However, conversing with the band when there is nothing for them to promote opens them up to more unguarded discussion, and offers some real moments, including a lovers' tiff between James and Nicky in the recording studio, and the band's drummer (and in my opinion the hero of *No Manifesto*) Sean Moore touting his gun collection and practising his aim at a shooting range. It all adds up to a rather unglamorous, yet also unpretentious encounter. Also, focusing on more mature Manic Street Preachers, who are now accustomed to the media glare, means they provide honest, measured, and funny responses to the questions. Compare James Dean Bradfield's twitchy interviews prior to *Everything Must Go*'s release with his relaxed manner in *No Manifesto*. Chalk and cheese.

A criticism that could be fired at *No Manifesto* is that it simply does not delve deep enough or add up to much in the end. Though what a documentary that fully uncovers Manics culture would look like, and how long it would need to be, is difficult to fathom. Volumes, no doubt. The most definitive biography of the band, Simon Price's comprehensive *Everything: A Book About Manic Street Preachers* (1999), runs past 300 pages and just covers the first five albums. An updated edition, taking in all subsequent records, would possibly be as bulky as the real *Holy Bible*. Translated to an in-depth documentary, you would be talking about years of footage. Also, the film seems content to finish just as Edward's final testament, *Journal for Plague Lovers* (2009) is imminent. Their recording with seasoned producer Steve Albini is overlooked, and their return to critical good graces with *Postcards from a Young Man*, *Rewind the Film*, and *Futurology* is left out completely. Something of a shame considering they rediscovered their enthusiasm for rock music and experimentation at this juncture.

As rock documentaries go, *No Manifesto* is certainly no *Cocksucker Blues, Dig!, Some Kind of Monster*, or *The Devil and Daniel Johnston*. But Manic Street Preachers have never been rock behemoths like The Rolling Stones or Metallica. They have never courted the sleazy shenanigans of The Dandy Warhols and The Brian Jonestown Massacre. They have never been an indie concern like Daniel Johnston. They have always walked a fine line between mainstream and alternative rock circuits, courteous at one instant and reactionary the next. Their style and music have been too schizophrenic for them to become megastars. What makes them stand apart has always been their intense connection with their fans, the emotional scope of the music, the intelligence and meaning behind the lyrics, and their political stance. *No Manifesto* perfectly illuminates those aspects. It is far from a perfect documentary, but then Manic Street Preachers have always been far from a perfect band. That is why we love them.

CHAPTER SEVEN
Art for the Masses (2007-2013)

There was a sense of rejuvenation to Manic Street Preachers upon their return in 2007. The defeats of *Know Your Enemy* and *Lifeblood* were keenly felt, but so were the triumphs of their epic live shows and the creative reach of Wire and Bradfield's solo work. If being in a band had been a drag in those first few years of the new millennium, then some time apart had obviously been required to re-spark the magic.

The first rumblings of Manic Street Preachers new music came in the form of a limited 7 inch and download single titled Underdogs. The song was intended to address the fans or "the freaks" who had remained devoted to the band in spite of the strange anomaly of albums like *Know Your Enemy* and *Lifeblood*. Daniel W. in his article for *Vulture Hound* states that "There's always been a bit of an underdog mentality with both the band and its fan base, and in this track we get a real and meaningful fan anthem."[21] W. wasn't incorrect.

With its chugging guitars and thumping drum rolls, all indications were that the band had tapped back into that sense of glamour and spunk and had made them so thrilling to fans in the first place. It seemed likely that the band were rewarding fans, rather than exploring new sonic avenues.

Single 34:
Underdogs

Released: 19th March 2007; UK Chart Position: n/a
(1000 copies limited edition), Label: Columbia;
Album: *Send Away the Tigers*
B-sides: n/a
Producer: Dave Eringa

The sense of rejuvenation would be felt keenly on the next release from the forthcoming record. Titled Your Love Alone Is Not Enough and released on 23 April 2007, the song was a duet with Nina Persson of the band The Cardigans, and an anthem that reached incredible heights. What was surprising, although as we've previously discussed not at all surprising, was the utter pop sensibility of the composition. Even at their darkest, the Manics have snuck memorable melodies into the backbone of every song they've ever recorded. Your Love Alone... felt effortless, which for the Manics, it was.

The song featured a back and forth dialogue between Bradfield and Persson and when both voices came together the song seemed to fly away. The song also featured a brief Nicky Wire vocal ("I could've written all your lines"), which seemed perfectly reasonable.

Single 35:

Your Love Alone is Not Enough (ft. Nina Persson)
Released: 23rd April 2007; UK Chart Position: 2;
Label: Columbia; Album: *Send Away the Tigers*
B-sides: Boxes & Lists; Love Letter to the Future;
Welcome to the Dead Zone; Little Girl Lost;
Fearless Punk Ballad
Producer: Dave Eringa

The accompanying music video was one of the band's better attempts at the form. The video featured the Manics facing off against Persson and her all female band positioned on the opposite side of the room. As the song progresses the two platforms merge and all members perform the remainder of the song together.

The song entered the U.K charts at number 2. The song also saw considerable success across the globe, coming in at number 5 in Norway, number 7 in Belgium, and number 20 in New Zealand. It also reached a staggering number 10 in the now defunct European Hot 100 Singles, which compiled sales from sixteen European countries.

As comeback singles go, Your Love Alone... is a prime example. It reignited interest from the general public and reinvested the original fans in the sound the band were making. The single's success also worked for the band. Knowing that an audience was ready and willing to engage (or reengage) with them was essential.

Album 8

Send Away the Tigers
Released: 7th May 2007; UK Chart Position: 2; Label: Columbia
Track Listing: Send Away the Tigers; Underdogs; Your Love Alone Is Not Enough (ft. Nina Persson); Indian Summer; The Second Great Depression; Rendition; Autumnsong; I'm Just a Patsy; Imperial Bodybags; Winterlovers (includes hidden track Working Class Hero by John Lennon)
Producers: Dave Eringa, Greg Haver, Loz Williams

On 7th May 2007, Manic Street Preachers eighth studio record, titled *Send Away the Tigers* was issued. Reviews for the record from critics and fans were extremely positive. Many noted that the record felt like a return to form, or a back to basics approach of writing steady guitar driven anthems in the vein of Guns N' Roses. It was certainly a relief to hear songs like the opening Send Away the Tigers, the riotous Imperial Bodybags, the pumping Rendition, and the lark of I Am Just a Patsy. The whole record felt effortless in their execution of riffs and melody. It felt very much like the band were not fighting against their own pop sensibility.

But to say *Send Away the Tigers* was a return to form, is to discredit the previous records. Sure, the band had found their sense of drama and flamboyance, but, as we've discussed *Know Your Enemy* and *Lifeblood* offered the band new audio adventures and new options in where the band could go. They may have been earnest and took it way too seriously, but these records matter. Any record the Manics have and will go on to make should be considered an evolution in their sound.

Of course, this is all in retrospect. No one was thinking of this when *Send Away the Tigers* landed. A wave of relief at having a good time rock and roll band who were willing to embrace their silliness was what most were thinking and feeling.

The record stormed in at number 2 in the U.K album charts and charted in the top 50 across Europe and in far flung places like Japan and New Zealand.

Send Away the Tigers doesn't shy away from the band's past. In fact, it openly embraces it. Clocking in at just ten tracks, plus a bonus hidden cover of John Lennon's Working Class Hero (did they *really* laugh when Lennon was shot?), and with an austere running time of just under forty minutes (*Know Your Enemy* had cloaked in a seventy-five-minute runtime), the record feels closer to the Manics of the *Gold Against the Soul* era. That record had also been a solid ten tracks that vied for the radio-friendliness of AOR rock. Any song from *Send Away the Tigers* could have sat comfortably on a mainstream radio playlist.

Send Away the Tigers and its subsequent singles would all feature images taken from Valerie Phillips 2005 book *Monika Monster Future First Woman on Mars,* which gave the releases a unified aesthetic similar to the *Know Your Enemy* releases that were designed by Welsh artist Neale Howells Whilst this record and the era of the band is fondly remembered, it's also frustrating that chugging politically-charged anthems like Imperial Bodybags, and Rendition sat as album tracks and didn't get their chance to shine as singles. Instead the band issued Autumnsong, which wasn't in any way a bad choice, just an obvious one. The song sours up on a Slash inspired riff with lyrics that ask "Now baby, what've you done to your hair?"

<u>Single 36:</u>

Autumnsong
Released: 23rd July 2007, UK Chart Position: 10;
Label: Columbia; Album: *Send Away the Tigers*
B-sides: Red Sleeping Beauty (McCarthy cover);
The Long Goodbye; Morning Comrades; The
Vorticists
Producer: Dave Eringa

Bizarrely, the single featured two different music videos. Neither one particularly sells the song well. The first featured a group of teenagers hanging around together in various urban locations. The other was shot by photographer Valerie Phillips at the band's request after seeing the first video and being disappointed in the outcome. Phillips' video features a one shot take of the two girls from *Send Away the Tigers* album cover (Monika Monster and her cousin Kate) awkwardly miming along to the song and unenthusiastically air-guitaring against a plain white background.

The next single release from *Send Away the Tigers* was the quite wonderful Indian Summer, released on October 1, 2007. The song stole the waltz-style signature from A Design for Life, but instead of addressing the working-class social structure opted for a reminisce of the band's youth. The single charted at number 22, breaking an eleven year run of top twenty singles. Indian Summer's music video was a collaboration with Wire's brother Patrick Jones and featured the band playing a bit of footy on a stone beach and eating a bag of chips on a pier.

Single 37:

Indian Summer
Released: October 1, 2007, UK Chart Position: 22,
Label: Columbia; Album: *Send Away the Tigers*
B-sides: Anorexic Rodin; Heyday of The Blood;
Foggy Eyes (Beat Happening cover); Lady Lazarus;
You Know It's Going to Hurt
Producers: Dave Eringa, Greg Haver

Indian Summer would mark the moment when the single format would begin to fade out and become less relevant. Changes in music were afoot and band's like the Manics who had always put together good single packages would see them become obsolete in the very near future.

Send Away the Tigers was just an excellent collection of songs. No real unifying message behind the album existed, except the realization that the Manics were having fun once again.

Perhaps what really becomes apparent in this small era of the band's history was the sheer quality of songs they were writing and producing. All the singles from *Send Away the Tigers* featured two or three B-sides that stood out as truly brilliant songs in their own right.

Your Love Alone... featured five songs spread out across it's numerous formats that would have sat comfortably as singles themselves. Boxes & Lists, Welcome to The Deadzone, Little Girl Lost, Love Letter to The Future, and the Smashing Pumpkins-esq Fearless Punk Ballad all came with memorable tunes and great lyrics. Autumnsong featured the B-sides The Long Goodbye, which had Wire taking up lead vocals, and the acoustic Morning Comrades and 1404. The final single, Indian Summer featured the blistering Anorexic Roden, the short and punchy Heyday of the Blood, the instrumental You Know This Is Going to Hurt, and the Wire sung Lady Lazarus.

Cover versions also appeared on these single formats and showed the band re-connecting with their past and having fun. The band's cover of McCarthy's Red Sleeping Beauty couldn't quite match the strident beauty of the original, but still held some power, whilst their cover of Beat Happening's Foggy Eyes was silly yet inspired.

Single 38:

The Ghosts of Christmas
Released: 1st December 2007, UK Chart Position:
n/a (free download non-chart eligible) Label:
Columbia
B-Sides: n/a
Producer: Dave Eringa

To wrap up a great year, the Manics released
their first (and to this point only) Christmas single.
Released as a free download via the band's website,
The Ghost of Christmas was described by Marc
Burrows in *Drowned in Sound* "a full on, sax-drenched
glam rock"[22] banger. There really is no other
description. The band threw sleigh-bells, saxophones,
big guitars and drums at the wall to create the feeling
of excitement that a young kid and their sleep
deprived parents on Christmas morning can only feel.

Where to go next? Manic Street Preachers had
returned to find themselves in a similar position to
ten years previous after the release of *Everything
Must Go*. Popular, award-winning, bestselling, and
fiercely intelligent as ever. It seemed reasonable that
the band would not rid themselves of the good will
awarded to them. It seemed very likely they would
continue in the same vein as *Send Away the Tigers*
and make good ol' fashion rock and roll anthems
drenched in melody and swarveness.

Album 9

Journal for Plague Lovers
Released: 18th May 2009, UK Chart Position: 3;
Label: Columbia

Track Listing: Peeled Apples; Jackie Collins Existential Question Time; Me and Stephen Hawking; This Joke Sport Severed; Journal for Plague Lovers; She Bathed Herself in a Bath of Bleach; Facing Page: Top Left; Marlon J.D.; Doors Closing Slowly; All Is Vanity; Pretension/Repulsion; Virginia State Epileptic Colony; William's Last Words (lyrics by Edwards, music by Bradfield, Wire, and Moore)

Producers: Steve Albini, Dave Eringa

By now one must realize that the Manics rarely play by 'the rules' that have bestowed legions of other bands.

Journal for Plague Lovers was the band's ninth studio album and one that contained all lyrics penned by Richey Edwards, the band's former lyricist and guitarist. Weeks before Edwards had disappeared, he had handed over a binder of lyrics and imagery to his band mates to peruse over the 1994 Christmas period. These were intended to be used on the next Manic Street Preachers record, a follow-up to *The Holy Bible*.

With Edwards' disappearance, this binder of lyrics took on a deeper meaning for the remaining band members, one that could not be fully understood in the immediate aftermath of such a harrowing event.

So, rather than follow-up the triumphalism of *Send Away the Tigers* with another bash of glamorous rock & roll, the band decided it was time to revisit those remaining lyrics penned by Richey Edwards.

This was a masterstroke. Released at any other time, a record that trod on old ground could have been accused of a cash-in. But coming after *Send*

Away the Tigers, *Journal for Plague Lovers* sits more as an isolated artistic act in the band's catalogue than an actual proper record in the narrative arc of the band.

With distance, it also cannot be considered a follow-up to the dark and troubled *The Holy Bible*. In fact, considering the set of lyrics contained on *Journal* was written around the same time, it shares very little in musical style or subject matter.

There was, for example, not much humour or hope to be found on *The Holy Bible* (although Manics fans might find grim hilarity in songs like Revol or Ifwhiteamericatoldthetruthforonedayit'sworldwould fallapart). Songs like Archives of Pain (pro-death penalty), 4st 7lbs (pro-anorexia) and Intense Humming of Evil (subject: The Holocaust) offered little in the way of laughs. This cannot be said for *Journal*. The song Me and Stephen Hawking is one long in-joke that even features a proper joke in the line "Overjoyed me and Stephen Hawking we laughed / we missed the sex revolution when we failed the physical."

The sheer audacity of songs like Peeled Apples which feature impenetrable couplets like "Riderless horses, Noam Chomsky's Camelot" and "A dwarf takes his cockerel out of the cockfight" are utterly absurd yet provide thankful light relief. Then there is that cheeky repeated refrain found in Jackie Collins Existential Question Time of "Oh mummy, what's a sex pistol?" Oh, how we laughed! *Journal for Plague Lovers* has moments of light humour. Not many albums that spill from the Manics can claim the same.

But it is really the contemplative hope that permeates *Journal* that is most apparent and sets it aside from its spiritual predecessor. *The Holy Bible* offered little of this in its claustrophobic worldview. This record is different. The lyrical content of a song like This Joke Sport Severed might not radiate much warmth lyrically, but its musical complement of strummed acoustic guitar suddenly breaks into the most beautiful orchestration the Manics have set to record (and the Manics know a thing or two about drenching their songs in strings). The mood shifts from dour to the clouds breaking and the sunshine pouring through.

Perhaps the most hopeful song on the record comes in the form of what might be considered its most defeatist. William's Last Words must be considered a parting shot, a goodbye note of sorts. Lyrics such as "Wish me some luck as you wave goodbye to me" would certainly indicate the desire of its author to leave his life behind. Yet the song conjures up some beautiful imagery, such as the opening line of "Isn't it lovely, when the dawn brings the dew?" that whilst eternally sad, at least allows for the possibility of a new dawn. The standout line of "I'm really tired / I'd love to go to sleep and wake up happy," whilst defeatist, offers the listener hope that there is the desire from its author to at least awaken and continue on in some way.

There are some obvious pointers to *The Holy Bible*. Firstly, the record's artwork is produced by the same British artist, Jenny Saville. The work that adorned *The Holy Bible*, titled *Strategy (South Face/Front Face/North Face)*, showed the same obese partially naked woman from three different angles, the expression on her face was of disgust. The artwork perfectly suited the record's dour view of humanity and the accusatory nature of that record ("Who's responsible? You fucking are.") *Journal*'s artwork, titled *Stare*, shows what appears to be a close-up of a young, though androgynous, girl, bruised and bewildered. It is a startling image and one that brought the band some controversy when UK supermarkets refused to display the record without a covering sleeve.

Another aspect that points back to *The Holy Bible* is the muted production. From 1996 onwards, the Manics (except for *Know Your Enemy*) had been known to produce lush and polished compositions. For *Journal*, the band roped in famed producer and recording engineer Steve Albini, whose work on countless indie records is overshadowed somewhat by his recording of Nirvana's third record *In Utero*. Albini's in-studio methodology is to simply record bands playing live. The sound produced on *Journal* certainly conjures up a rougher audio experience, dispensing with the lavish sheen of earlier records and stripping back to a more basic and bombastic sound.

So, what is *Journal for Plague Lovers*?

Is it an attempt to relive past glories of once furious youth? The exploitation of a past band member who was missing, presumed dead, and therefore unable to comment on or guide the music and overall artistic outcome in any way, shape, or form? Is it an attempt to re-spark the creative flow and boost declining record sales?

It is none of these things. The record is strange, though welcome. An anomaly that exists outside of Manic Street Preachers' regular releases, yet is also a part of it. Whilst it cannot outperform its towering spiritual partner, *The Holy Bible*, nor does it quite equal the lyrical tirades of that record, it makes for an intriguing complement and adds layers to the darkness that existed within that record. It adds dimensions of lightness and hope to an otherwise hopeless perception of humanity, and depth to a lyricist and icon who is still sadly missed.

Critically acclaimed and adored by fans, Manic Street Preachers couldn't seem to put a foot wrong. The start of the millennium had seen the band try on some new tactics, but the critical backlash and the dwindling sales had meant they returned to what they did best: crack out top melodies, striking lyrics, and mind boggling guitar riffs. *Journal for Plague Lovers* had been a project that had referenced their past and the sound they created for that record was more abrasive and in line with its spiritual predecessor *The Holy Bible*. Yet this swerve didn't concern many. It seemed natural that a follow-up to *Send Away the Tigers* and *Journal for Plague Lovers* might try to mix the two.

When *Postcards from a Young Man* was announced in the early summer of 2010, James Dean Bradfield had stated that the record was "one last shot at mass communication".[23] It was noble that the Manics, so late into their career, were still willing and energized enough to consider the possibility of pulling in some new listeners. Nicky Wire followed up Bradfield's comment with "It was a conscious decision this time to want to hear ourselves on the radio. Our mantra at the start was, 'If you've got something to say, say it to as many people as possible'."[24]

The Manics frame of mind seemed to be in the same state as their debut record twenty years previously: sneak the intellectual garb on the back of pop rock melodies.

So it's somewhat unfortunate to address *Postcards from a Young Man* as a failure to live up to the standards set by the band. It wasn't the music per say that was the issue, although we'll get to that in short order. But the changes in the music industry meant and the way people were consuming music didn't quite gel with the band's continued standard operating procedure of single, album, tour, that they had relied on. The older fans were in rapture of course, newer fans were probably harder to come by in the new musical environment.

<hr>

<u>Single 39:</u>

(It's Not War) Just the End of Love
Released: 13th September 2010; UK Chart Position: 28; Label: Columbia; Album: *Postcards from a Young Man*
B-sides: I'm Leaving You for Solitude; Distractions; Ostpolitik; Lost Voices; I Know the Numbers
Producer: Dave Eringa

<hr>

The first flush of new sounds from the forthcoming album came on 13 September 2010 the form of the first single release titled (It's Not War) Just the End of Love. The NME called the song "an age-appropriate renewal of their destroy-culture manifesto" and "quite literally the daftest, campest, most outlandish stadium pop song the Manics have ever put their minds to"[25] It was a fair assessment of a song that made no qualms about how flamboyant it was.

The song's music video featured a slow-motion one-shot take of actors Michael Sheen and Anna Friel playing chess before jumping on the chess table and making out. The members of the band, dressed in sober suits and ties, look on in bored bemusement.

The Manics tenth record, *Postcards from a Young Man*, landed on 20 September 2010. As Wire had proclaimed a few months prior, it was a galient attempt to entice a wider audience. Big chorus, lush melodies, stirring strings, outrageous riffs, gospel choirs, yes you read that right, a gospel choir appears on four of twelve songs. Guest musicians, from Guns 'n' Roses' bass player Duff MacKeigan to Echo and the Bunnymen's vocalist Ian McCulloch appear. *Postcards from a Young Man* was an ambitious record, a sign that the band, twenty years into their mainstream career and ten records in, were happy to test themselves and their audience.

<u>Album 10:</u>

Postcards from a Young Man
Released: 20th September 2010; UK Chart Position: 3; Label: Columbia
Track Listing: (It's Not War) Just the End of Love; Postcards from a Young Man; Some Kind of Nothingness (ft. Ian McCulloch); The Descent (Pages 1 & 2); Hazelton Avenue; Auto-Intoxication (ft. John Cale); Golden Platitudes; I Think I Found It; A Billion Balconies Facing the Sun (ft. Duff McKagan); All We Make Is Entertainment; The Future Has Been Here 4Ever; Don't Be Evil
Producers: Dave Eringa, Loz Williams, Manic Street Preachers

Postcards from a Young Man feels ambitious for sure, yet its musical direction is as pointed out in Andrzej Lukowski's review for *Drowned in Sound* "a foray into Seventies-style AOR and power-pop". Lukowski also points out quite rightly that the "polished retro pop doesn't ultimately play to the strong suits of a band who thrive on anger, anthems and the odd bit of absurdity."[26]

This is the ultimate fate of the record. By trying to sound like the tame 'normie' songs on the radio, the Manics somehow lost their spark. *Postcards from a Young Man* is almost exactly what Motown Junk was raging against all those years ago. Plain, soulless, derivative pop music. The Manics were better than this, surely?

But always a band committed to an album's grand thesis, the band released the single Some Kind of Nothingness on 6 December 2010. The song was a pleasant enough duet with Ian McCulloch, which soured to a rousing gospel chorus towards the end. The band had long loved Echo and the Bunnymen and they have even been James Dean Bradfield's first live experience way back in the mid-1980s.

Single 40:

Some Kind of Nothingness
Released: 6th December 2010; UK Chart Position: 44; Label: Columbia; Album: *Postcards from a Young Man*
B-sides: Broken Up Again; Red Rubber; Evidence Against Myself; Slow Reflections/Strange Delays; Time Ain't Nothing; Masses Against the Classes (Live); Sleepflower (Live) [lyrics by Edwards and Wire, music by Bradfield and Moore]; Yes (Live) [lyrics by Edwards and Wire, music by Bradfield and Moore]
Producer: Dave Eringa

What is more interesting about the song is that it is a full Nicky Wire composition in lyrics and music. In this sense, the song is quite an extraordinary accomplishment and quite a step ahead from Wire's debut solo record of punkish dirges. This can even be witnessed in the quite wonderful Wire-led demo version of the song that appeared on the deluxe edition of the record (it's also on YouTube). Stripped of the strings, McCulloch's and Bradfield's more flashy vocal styles, and the gospel choir, the song has a beautiful yearning quality that has been lost in translation to the recorded version.

To promote the song the band decked themselves out in flash suits and played the song on the immensely popular show *Strictly Come Dancing*. With that kind of exposure and the song's uplifting nature, Some Kind of Nothingness should have been a bonafide mega-hit. Instead the song stalled at number 44 in the singles chart. This was the band's first single in almost twenty years that hadn't managed to break into the top forty. Always a good statistician, Nicky Wire informed *Absolute Radio* that "I was quite distraught that our single missed the Top 40. I was gutted."[27]

Personal opinion will have to suffice here, but I recall at the time of this single's failure to chart in the top forty being somewhat relieved. I had been disappointed in the direction the band had taken in trying to appease a mass audience when clearly their artistic and commercial triumph with *Journal for Plague Lovers* had shown that the band could survive the new musical environment just fine with a tweak to how they make and release records. Chasing for hit singles and radio play in an age where these things were becoming less important seemed retroactive.

That opinion seemed justified by low performing singles, despite the effort made to promote them.

In the intervening years, *Postcards from a Young Man* still stands out as a weird anomaly among the band's discography. Of course, it shouldn't be the case. It should've been the biggest hit of their later career. In a readers' poll conducted by the music website *Albumism*, *Postcards from a Young Man* sits at number 11, or third from bottom in the band's releases.[28] Of course, it has to stand against the mighty *The Holy Bible* and *Everything Must Go* and the earlier more defining releases, but the band's more recent record, *Resistance is Futile* sits comfortably just above it.

This isn't to suggest that *Postcards from a Young Man* is an empty gesture. A record, that in its desire to be embraced by all, doesn't have something to say. The singles that were released don't quite reflect the experimental and political nature of the record. The Manics still knew how to write a good song that reflected on lost ideologies as witnessed on the Wire composition Golden Platitudes, which Wire reflects was "about the abandonment of the true working class by their own party, the nadir for me being when New Labour offered everyone a free laptop. So insulting, so metropolitan."[29] And how about the spiky Don't Be Evil and A Billion Balconies Facing the Sun. Both these songs grapple with the rise of technology and the movement of social interactions from the physical to the virtual. Not many bands or artists were writing about this in 2010.

> ### Single 41:
>
> Postcards from a Young Man
> Released: 28th February 2011; UK Chart Position:
> 54; Label: Columbia: Album: *Postcards from a
> Young Man*
> B-sides: Inky Fingers; Engage with Your Shadow;
> Kiss My Eyes for Eternity; Midnight Sun; The
> Passing Show; This Joke Sport Severed (live);
> Peeled Apples (live); Marlon J.D. (live)
> Producer: Dave Eringa

To send the album off, the band released the titular track from the record on 28 February 2011. Whilst it performed well during the week of release and cracked the top forty, the song fell to number 54 when the charts were announced the following week.

Despite being and indeed remaining a classic singles band, and one of the top-selling acts in the UK, Manic Street Preachers would find themselves absent from the top forty for the remainder of the decade. The changes in music consumption and the preferred genres meant that what might be called traditional rock or alternative rock was kept out of the top forty in favour of musical styles such as pop, grime, hip-hop and EDM. This music was intended for the audience who streamed and downloaded their music as opposed to buying the physical formats.

> ### Single 42:
>
> This is the Day
> Released: 18th September 2011, UK Chart Position:
> n/a (limited edition); Label: Columbia; Album:
> National Treasures

B-sides: We Were Never Told; This Is the Day;
Rock 'n' Roll Genius
Producers: Loz Williams & Manic Street Preachers

As previously discussed, the last Manic Street Preachers hits compilation, *Forever Delayed* had edited out some of the band's more obtuse moments and placed the order of the songs in a strange non-linear narrative that meant songs that were worlds apart in style, rubbed awkwardly next to one another. What was needed was a good collection of the defining singles and N*ational Treasures – The Complete Singles* was it. Released on 31 October 2011, just as the Christmas shopping began, the collection placed all the singles neatly in chronological order. There was an air of celebration about the collection. Whilst *Forever Delayed*, had felt like a full stop in their career, and at that point the full stop could really have been the end of a chapter or an end of the book, *National Treasures* felt like a continuation. Much more was to come from the band's development, and these songs had played their part in that development. The term National Treasure was fitting. Not only had these songs become ingrained in the national consciousness and literally treasured, the band members themselves had become icons of British music and culture.

To continue the mood of celebration the band performed all the hit singles at The O2 Arena (formerly the Millennium Dome) on 17th December 2011. A cracking way to end this part of their career.

CHAPTER EIGHT
The Sense of the Familiar (2014-present)

Manic Street Preachers next recorded endeavour would depart from their style and sound of previous efforts in a remarkable way and point towards a pretty exciting future. The album, *Rewind the Film* would be released on 16 September 2013 and with it news that another album was already in the bag and awaiting release. In an act of incredible creative drive, the band had embedded themselves in their Faster Studios and made excursions to Rockfield in Monmouthshire and Hansa in Berlin to work on a collection of thirty-five songs that spanned a wide range of diversity. Nicky Wire in *Walesonline* shared the distinct nature of both records: "One will be more acoustic and gentle in nature with lots of horns and a real Atlantic soul element to it, while the other's going to be way more spikey with lots and lots of electric guitar on there."[30]

Rewind the Film would see the band embrace their age and status as British rock's elder statesmen. But, despite its curmudgeon elements and laid back approach, the record creates a world of its own which seems to make perfect sense.

Single 43:

Show Me the Wonder
Released: 9th September 2013; UK Chart Position: 77; Label: Columbia; Album: *Rewind the Film*
B-sides: Melancholyme; Tsunami (live); T.E. Lawrence on a Bike; What Happened to the Blue Generation

---

I've always seen *Rewind the Film* as a visual record. Possibly more so than any other of their past releases, at least from the last decade of their career. This certainly has something to do with the collaboration with Welsh filmmaker Keiran Evans. Evans had worked within the music industry for years, directing music videos and documentaries for the likes of Kyle Minogue and Saint Etienne. His directorial debut film *Kelly + Victor* won the BAFTA Award for Outstanding Debut by a British Writer, Director or Producer at the 2014 awards ceremony. Evans then went on to put together a seventy-two-minute documentary for the twentieth anniversary of the Manics debut album which was titled *Culture, Alienation, Boredom and Despair.* This began Evans' lengthy collaboration with the band and one of their most successful visual interpretations of their career.

The first song to be heard from *Rewind the Film* was the titular song. Though not released as an official single, the track offered the listener a good indication of where the record was heading and the ideas of introspection it wanted to explore.

Starting off with a lovely David Axelrod based acoustic guitar sample the song builds towards a sense of nostalgia. Of course, the most startling thing about *Rewind the Film* was the fact that the tones of James Dean Bradfield were replaced by English singer-songwriter, and guitarist, Richard Hawley. Hawley had made a name for himself as a member of the British band The Longpigs and later Pulp. He had also released solo material and collaborated with artists as diverse as Paul Weller, Arctic Monkeys, Nancy Sinatra, and Lisa Marie Presley. Hawley's connection to the Manics came when he, Bradfield and Wire wrote songs for Welsh singer Shirley Bassey in 2009. The Manics had written the song The Girl from Tiger Bay for inclusion on Bassey's record *The Performance*. Hawley had written the song After the Rain.

The sense of nostalgia created by *Rewind the Film* is pushed even further by Kieran Evans' exquisite video for the song that shows an old geezer opening and clearing up an old working men's club in the Rhondda Valley in Wales. The empty hall and disused equipment from games of bingo and live performances show an era long gone. As a kid who grew up very close to a working men's club that was bulldozed and replaced with expensive private housing, I'm aware of the importance these spaces offered the community, the solidarity and closeness they provided, and the sense of loss felt when they finally closed. As a kid, I'd accompany my dad to the local WMC. Whilst he opted for a decent pint, a good chat, a bag of crisps and a chance at the 'fruity' machine, I'd meet up with other kids from the estate and drop 50p in the arcade machines, whilst necking a bottle of pop. It wasn't fancy, but it brought the community together in a positive sense.

The actual first single from *Rewind the Film* dropped on September 9, 2013. Show Me The Wonder was a rousing brass band led number that was among the most jaunty the Manics had ever written. The Evans directed video took the band back to the heyday of the working men's club era. Decked out in lovely suits, stuck on sideburns and seventies-tastic moustaches, the band played the song whilst a group of young teens danced and flirted on the dancefloor.

The Manics have often written songs that
longed for youth and the more innocent time of the
past. This has been based on the personal
experiences of growing up in Wales, but also the
more black and white/left and right experiences of
politics as well. The songs Rewind the Film and Show
Me The Wonder, with their visuals directed by Evans
perfectly encapsulates the feeling of memory and
loss.

And this memory and loss would dominate
Rewind the Film as a whole. The whole record could
be easily summarized by Frank Sinatra's famous
recording of My Way ("regrets, I've had a few") in
that it paints an individual, in this case Wire, as
broken, disenfranchised, disconnected and
introspective. Clues were in titles such as This Sullen
Welsh Heart, 3 Ways to See Despair, and Running Out
of Fantasy. In many ways *Rewind the Film* shares its
defeatist nature with *This is My Truth Tell Me Yours*.
That record is devoid of hope, but what is apparent

on *Rewind the Film* is the knowledge and acknowledgement that these middle stages of life still hold wonder, happiness and light in even the face of adversity.

Single 44:

Anthem for a Lost Cause
Released: 25th November 2013; UK Chart Position: 200; Label: Columbia: Album: *Rewind the Film*
B-sides: Death of a Digital Ghost; See It Like Sutherland; She Is Suffering (live) [lyrics by Edwards and Wire, music by Bradfield and Moore]
Producers: Loz Williams, Manic Street Preachers

One more single would be released from the record, the Bradfield composed Anthem for a Lost Cause. Again the short visual accompaniment again came from the hand of Kieran Evans and continued the story of the teens seen in the Show Me The Wonder video. Taking place a few years later and at the height of the miners' strike, the video follows the perspective of the wives and partners of the striking workers as they dealt with the bleak situation they faced. Evans commented that women during the strike were essential in bringing the community together and in fact: "represented the very essence of true socialist principles; collectivising and organising themselves not only to protest against the huge injustice they suffered at the hands of Thatcher but also to feed, clothe and support fellow their fellow workers and their families"[31]

The final track on *Rewind the Film* offered some small clues that the fire in the band's belly had not been fully extinguished. The song, 30 Year War, was a scathing attack on the "endless parade of old, Etonian scum" of the British Tories and their continued assault on the lives of the working class through policy and austerity measures that "Keep 'em boxed in, keep 'em kettled in". Lyrically speaking, it was fun to hear an attack on the British establishment that could have nestled itself neatly on the band's debut album.

Single 45:

Walk Me to The Bridge
Released: 28th April 2014; UK Chart Position: 86;
Label: Columbia: Album: *Futurology*
B-sides: The Sound of Detachment; Caldey
Producers: Loz Williams, Alex Silva

Rewind the Film feels not unlike a full stop in the band's career. More laid back, less flashy, more introspective and sullen. It saw the band in critical good graces and even though the singles didn't get anywhere near the top forty, the album had peaked at number four in the UK charts. Respectable in the age of download and streaming.

If retirement was on the band's agenda, it wouldn't have been a huge shock. Nicky Wire could have retired to write his memoirs and concentrate on his Polaroid based artworks. James Dean Bradfield could have become a legendary session player or, as we'd soon discover in 2019, a great podcast host. Sean Moore could have become a wry Twitter critic and technology journalist. The record could have easily acted as a final and graceful farewell from the old commie stalwarts who had come to the conclusion that changes couldn't be made so why bother anyway.

Of course there was always an awareness that *Rewind the Film* would be followed-up in short order, and the band's twelfth album, *Futurology*, landed on 7 July 2014.

What was remarkable about the record was the obvious difference to *Rewind the Film*. The record seemed to embrace the idea of new possibilities and new horizons. The band's musical approach was brazen and open. It was difficult to imagine the band recording the songs that appeared on *Rewind the Film* and *Futurology* at the same moment. The works are miles apart.

This was evidenced on the first single to be issued from *Futurology*. Titled Walk Me to The Bridge and released on 28 April 2014, the song begins with a minimalist bass structure which soon erupts into a classic euphoric Manics chorus. Nicky Wire shared what the song was about with *Gigwise*, stating that "It's about the idea of bridges allowing you an out of body experience as you leave and arrive in different places."[32]

Album 12:

Futurology
Released: 7th July 2014; UK Chart Position: 2; Label: Columbia
Track Listing: Futurology; Walk Me to the Bridge; Let's Go to War; The Next Jet to Leave Moscow (ft. Cian Ciaran); Europa Geht Durch Mich (ft. Nina Hoss); Divine Youth (ft. Georgia Ruth); Sex, Power, Love and Money; Dreaming a City (Hughesovka); Black Square; Between the Clock and the Bed (ft.

Green Gartside); Misguided Missile; The View from Stow Hill; Mayakovsky
Producers: Alex Silva, Loz Williams, Manic Street Preachers

With *Rewind the Film* feeling like an album that might want to stay home with a pipe and comfy slippers, *Futurology* felt like an album wanting to embrace travel, art, architecture, and revolution. It was, quite honestly, the Manics at their most optimistic.

Futurology also contains a sense of musical adventurism. Synths and samples appear as well as an array of guest vocalists, the most startling of which is German actress Nina Hoss singing in her native tongue on the song Europa Geht Durch Mich. The pounding beat and siren squeals of guitar that marches Europa Geht Durch Mich on creates the band's most militant and tight composition since Faster.

As well as Nina Hoss, there was also a lovely duet between Bradfield and Scritti Politti frontman Green Gartside on the song Between the Clock and The Bed, and Welsh singer and harpist Georgia Ruth on the achingly beautiful Wire composition Divine Youth. Despite its desire to look towards Europe for inspiration *Futurology* marks the band's most collaborative record with an array of Welsh musicians joining in on the chanted chorus of Let's Go to War, and Super Furry Animals keyboardist Cian Ciarán tinkling the keys on the songs Futurology and The Next Jet to Leave Moscow.

The album went into the UK album charts at number 2, two places above *Rewind the Film*. Another single was also issued in the form of the album's title song and one that best summarized *Futurology* as a whole. Described by the *NME* as a song that "serves as a manifesto for all that follows: a declaration of positivity."[33]

Single 46:

Futurology
Released: 22nd September 2014; UK Chart Position; n/a; Label: Columbia; Album: *Futurology*
B-sides: Antisocialmanifesto; Kodawari
Producers: Loz Williams, Manic Street Preachers

Both the singles that came from *Futurology* continued the collaboration with director Kairan Evans who matched the songs with cinematic short films that fitted wonderfully with the records wide scope. The film that accompanied Walk Me to The Bridge for example was an update on the theme of the 1998 German film *Run Lola Run*, which sees a young woman pacing through urban spaces in a race against time.

After the release of two records within the space of a year, it wouldn't be a huge surprise to see the band take a break and reflect. Reflection was certainly on the cards as the band faced a number of anniversaries of albums and events. No one was quite prepared for the amount of coverage the band would give to the twentieth anniversary edition of *The Holy Bible*. The tenth anniversary in 2004, had seen a wonderful reissue of the record, but, here, ten years later, the band seemed to have made some kind of peace with the record that had been such a traumatic experience at the time.

On 8th December 2014, the band reissued the record as a beautiful package that included heavyweight vinyl, four CDs that contained live recordings and B-sides and a 40-page booklet of photos and notes. Not only this, the band also decided to tour the anniversary, with dates in the UK and North America. The whole celebration concluded with an outdoor show at Cardiff Castle in which the band decked themselves out in military gear and raged through the album in chronological order. After a short interval, they arrived back on stage in their more sober attire and knocked out the hits. The whole concert was filmed by Kieran Evans and released as the "Anti-Concert Film" film *Be Pure, Be Vigilant, Behave.*

It was interesting that the view of T*he Holy Bible* was so radically different twenty years from its original release. Over the course of these two decades, only a handful of the songs had ever been played live and for the most part the band seemed uncomfortable talking about it and the surrounding era. Rightly so, one might think. The record itself offers a bleak overview of humanity, but the era also leads to the disappearance of Richey Edwards and the very likely disintegration of the band. For the listener, *The Holy Bible* offers a torrent of hatred and misery, for the band actually writing and playing those songs, the feeling must be tenfold. Here, the band performed the record almost as a macabre Cabaret act. In an ingenious way, the band turned this difficult record into a moment of cathartic theatre.

Single 47:

Together Stronger (C'mon Wales)

Released: 13th May 2016; UK Chart Position: 56
(iTunes Chart); Label: Sony; Album: n/a
B-sides: n/a
Producer: Dave Eringa

And so then came *Resistance is Futile*, the
thirteenth Manic Street Preachers record. Or, perhaps
that should be the twelfth, which if according to the
band's youthful pronouncements to make one great
record, that being 1992's *Generation Terrorists*, and
split up, should never have even existed. This slip
from the sharp and snarky tongue of bass player
Nicky Wire has haunted the band after almost every
subsequent record release in the last three decades.
Thankfully, the band has continued long enough to
drop this (and many previous) pop bombs on its
audience.

Resistance is Futile came four years after
Futurology, the band's last major record. That record
set a new precedent for the band as they embraced a
European sensibility of Krautrock and synthpop. The
record infused art movements with innovation in
sound and aesthetics. During these four years
between records, the band had celebrated
commemorative twentieth-anniversary reissues of
The Holy Bible and *Everything Must Go*, as well as
reissuing a tenth-anniversary edition of *Send Away
the Tigers*.

Barring perhaps 2009's *Postcards from a
Youngman* Manic Street Preachers barely made a
misstep in the last decade. Every record in this period
has felt like a winning formula of the band's vibrant
and sweeping melancholic anthems. When the band
first announced *Resistance is Futile* towards the end
of 2017 with the release of the vibrant single

International Blue, a song of thumping, sky-scraping beauty it felt like the run of good luck wasn't about to end any time soon.

And it did not. *Resistance is Futile* saw the Manic Street Preachers still in the throes of a creative pinnacle.

<u>Single 48:</u>

International Blue
Released: 8th December 2017; UK Chart Position: 39 (iTunes Chart), Label: Sony; Album: *Resistance is Futile*
B-sides: Holding Patterns
Producer: Dave Eringa

Let us look at that title. Thankfully it outlived the initial sniggers of the *Star Trek* connection (the title of the record is also the calling card of Star Trek's mighty nemesis The Borg, a species of techno-infused aliens) and became something more profound. There is a negative connotation in the title for sure. The resistance is towards modern living, to social media, to fake news, to Brexit, to Trump. Indeed, the band's own Faster Studio in Cardiff was bulldozed to make way for a block of stylish apartments; resistance is to the charge of modernity. Yet the stunning photograph of the Samurai Warrior that adorns the cover of the record symbolizes something brazen and strong. A vital last stand against whatever is coming next. The title is also a remark of the content of the record. Such musical and melodious devotion to each track means that every second seems irresistible to the ear.

Moving into the record it became clear the band had lost nothing when it came to hooks from which to hang their gorgeous and shimmering melodies. *Resistance is Futile* drives that point home harder than anything since 2007's *Send Away the Tigers*. There are call-backs to the past. This is to be expected and frankly welcome from a band who at the time of the recording was knocking on fifty years of age.

There is certainly evidence to back up that the band has tapped into their sense of nostalgia from time to time. Here it is far more subtle. International Blue and Distant Colours could have sat on *Everything Must Go* or *Postcards from a Young Man*. The mosh-inducing Broken Algorithms sounds like a direct pull from *Generation Terrorists* or, musically at least, *Journal for Plague Lovers*. Even in their earliest guise as stencil-bloused misanthropes, the band have longed for the past, ("the past is so beautiful/the future like a corpse in snow" — Condemned to Rock and Roll) why in middle-age and all the woes it brings would they wish to stop looking backward now?

A great aspect of any Manic Street Preachers record is the window into other worlds and cultural figures that the lyrical content of the songs provides. Here we are inundated with past lives. International

Blue concerns Yves Klein, the French painter who patented the colour of his own creation. Dylan and Caitlin, a wonderful duet with Catherine Anne Davies, known as The Anchoress give us insight into the turbulent relationship between Dylan and Caitlin Thomas. The song acts as one of the band's most successful duets since Your Love Alone Is Not Enough. Vivian is a peen to Vivian Maier, the nanny and street photographer whose work documented American urban life in superb and vivid detail yet was only discovered and celebrated posthumously. As with other figures the band has chosen to discuss in song (Kevin Carter, Paul Robeson) the compositions are simple snapshots of life that lead us towards a broader discovery.

Single 50:

Dylan & Caitlin
Released: 9th March 2018; UK Chart Position: n/a;
Label: Song; Album: *Resistance is Futile*
B-sides: n/a
Producer: Dave Eringa

One drawback of the record, though in some respects also its saving grace, is that there is no unifying theme or movement the record stands behind. In the past, Manic Street Preachers records have seen themselves as mini manifestos, redefining the band's ethos, or reacting against it. *Generation Terrorists* was an opening salvo, *The Holy Bible* a pre-millennial/anti-acceleration treatise, *Everything Must Go* was the euphoric comeback, same could also be said for *Send Away the Tigers*, *Rewind the Film* was a graceful yet existential look at aging, whilst

Futurology embraced European art movements and futurism. *Resistance is Futile* seems to have no such theme or collective point. Here we have a collection of songs, ones that identify themselves in different forms.

In this case, the record shares something with the band's second record, 1993's *Gold Against the Soul*. A record that contained some of the band's best and most loved songs (La Tristesse Durera, Roses in The Hospital, Sleepflower) but lacked a coherence awarded to the record that came before and those that came after. As mentioned, this is in some respects the record's saving grace. At the point in the record's cultural moment did we need yet another cause to stand behind? Manic Street Preachers address various discourses, and we are living in a moment of various issues. There is no one solution.

Single 51:

Liverpool Revisited
Released: 6th April 2018; UK Chart Position: n/a;
Label: Sony; Album: *Resistance is Futile*
B-sides: n/a
Producer: Dave Eringa

Album 13:

Resistance is Futile
Released: 13th April 2018; UK Chart Position: 2;
Label: Sony
Track Listing: People Give in; International Blue; Distant Colours (lyrics by Bradfield); Vivian; Dylan & Caitlin; Liverpool Revisited; Sequels of Forgotten Wars; Hold Me Like a Heaven; In Eternity; Broken

Algorithms; A Song for the Sadness; The Left
Behind
Producers: Dave Eringa, Gavin Fitzjohn, Guy
Massey

Single: 52:

Hole Me Like a Heaven
Released: 4th May 2018; UK Chart Position: n/a;
Label: Sony; Album: *Resistance is Futile*
B-sides: n/a
Producer: Dave Eringa

With *Resistance is Futile*, Manic Street
Preachers leaped forward once again. There were
elements of past endeavours, but the optimistic
sheen, the widescreen pomp, the inspiration taken
from art; poetry, landscape, political struggles and
divisions, and indeed hitting middle-age in a rock and
roll band give this record an edge that never lacks
conviction. The Manics might just have pulled off a
rarity: an album as vibrant and life-affirming as
anything in their history.

Single 53:

People Give In
Released: 27th July 2018; UK Chart Position: n/a;
Label: Sony; Album: *Resistance is Futile*
B-sides: n/a
Producer: Dave Eringa

Manic Street Preachers have spent their entire career writing songs that have shone a light on figures, events, and influences from the past. From Nixon to Nietzsche, Pol Pot to Public Enemy, Miller to Mailer, and Camus to The Clash. The references have always come thick and fast and offered the listener an escape hatch out of modern life and into a world populated by figures from history, philosophy, and culture. It seemed inevitable that eventually, the band would want to record an album dedicated to just one figure.

The opportunity arose not for the band as such, but as a second solo release for James Dean Bradfield during the lull period after the success of *Resistance is Futile*. Itching to get creative, Bradfield came across a set of poetry, plays, and writing exercises by Welsh poet and playwright Patrick Jones, who of course had a history with the band chiefly as Nicky Wire's older brother, but also as a collaborator with the band on numerous videos. Jones had also contributed several spoken word sections to *Generation Terrorists*, supplied the title (although it might be argued it was stolen) for the band's major comeback record *Everything Must Go*, and had been the opening act for their massive Manic Millennium concert in Cardiff.

The writings of Jones were all concerned in some way or another with the life and music of Chilean singer Victor Jara. Jara. Jara had been an avid supporter of Chile's democratically elected socialist president Salvador Allende, who was elected to power on 3 November 1970 but was overthrown and killed in a military coup on 11 September 1973 by General Augusto Pinochet. The persecution of those that had supported Allende and those that had been critical of Pinochet's harsh measures resulted in the executions of thousands of people. Jara was among those that were shepherded into Chile Stadium in Santiago (now named Estadio Víctor Jara) and then tortured and killed.

Bradfield's second solo release, titled *Even in Exile* was released on 14 August 2020 at the height of the Covid-19 health crisis. With live music on hold, Bradfield's release was a studio endeavour and a much welcome reprieve from the utter despair that inflicted the lives of almost everybody at the time. The record reached number 6 in the album charts.

CHAPTER NINE
The Blank Page Awaits

We have reached the end of the story, but the story is far from over.

As I write this, a new Manic Street Preachers record is on the way. Mooted song titles include Orwellian, Don't Let the Night Divide Us and Quest for Ancient Colour. The titles alone whet the appetite for new music from this band.

The new record is scheduled for a release sometime in 2021, depending how Covid-19 measures impact the recording. The band will also be taking to the stage for two nights at Cardiff Arena in July 2021 as a thank you and a fundraiser for the staff of the National Health Service who have worked to the point of exhaustion throughout 2020/21 with the Covid-19 health crisis. The two-night extravaganza was originally planned for December 2020, but the ongoing crisis has meant postponement. Depending on the outcome this event could very well be postponed again.

In light of James Dean Bradfield's second solo release, Nicky Wire is also said to be preparing a solo album. A record that according to Bradfield sounds "very modern, very electronic, and very soothsaying and prophetic."[34]

In some strange way, the future of the band seems more fixed and certain than it did in the backend of the 1990s. The band has overcome so much and prevailed so well that life without a forthcoming Manic Street Preachers record seems odd to both fans and to the band. The Manic Street Preachers have never shied away from the inevitable end of the band. You'll recall that as early as their 1991 debut record *Generation Terrorists* they were proclaiming in the music press that the record was to be their first and last statement. They would, after the record sold sixteen million copies and they had played a string of sold-out shows at Wembley Stadium, split up and never be seen again. *Generation Terrorists* did not achieve sixteen million and Wembley would not happen for a few years yet. During the slogging tour to promote the mega-selling *This is My Truth Tell Me Yours* in 1998/99 they confessed to an American interviewer that they were closer to the end of the band than the beginning. This, of course, would not be the case.

The concert that saw them say goodbye to the twentieth century at Cardiff's Millennium Stadium in front of an audience of 60,000 felt like an epoch, as if the band could call it quits then and there and walk away having achieved everything they ever set out to do. Of course, they marched on.

In the past decade, it has felt like each new record could be a signal towards an end. *Postcards from a Young Man* (2010) was an ambitious set of songs, and it was, as the band intended "one last shot at mass communication", a final attempt to see if they could pull off one last hurrah! *Rewind the Film* was the band's most subtle and sombre record, a reflection on years of emotional and physical turmoil being in a rock and roll band. The tone of the record could be akin to pulling up a nice cosy blanket and snoozing off for good. Yet its immediate follow-up *Futurology* felt like a fresh intake of air and a renewed sense of hope that the band might continue with renewed vigour. If it had finished there it would have been a satisfactory closing statement.

Resistance is Futile, the band's latest at the time of writing signalled that this could be the last record. The process of writing and recording *Resistance is Futile* was as Nicky Wire has suggested in numerous interviews, arduous, with the breakthrough only coming when International Blue blasted through like a ray of sunshine and suggested the direction the album should take. As a long-time fan of the band, I am still not done with them; I will probably never be done. I think I share this with the majority of fans who shape their lives around the band's record releases and tour dates, who live and breathe those lyrics and shiny choruses and travel extensive distances to old record shops in the hope of finding a rare vinyl EP or single in some dusty old display case. I have spent hours in contemplation about a future roster of records that still have to be fulfilled. To end this text on some fun and speculative way, I want to offer suggestions on where the band might still find expansion in sound.

A Nicky Wire-led Manic Street Preachers Album

In the past few years, Wire has taken the lead in writing lyrics and music for some of the band's best songs. Your Love Alone Is Not Enough, the comeback single from *Send Away the Tigers*, for which Wire wrote the music sparkled and shined like no other Manics track in quite some time. Marlon JD from *Journal for Plague Lovers* is a bristling number that comes from Wire's pen, whilst the Wire led The Future Has Been Here 4Ever from *Postcards from a Young Man* puts the Wire centre of a pumping rock anthem. Arguments could be made against Wire-led compositions such as Dying Breeds, Engage with Your Shadow, and Failure Bound as filler dross, but even these tracks show competence and experimentation that goes beyond the core Manics sound of the main albums. A Nicky Wire led album would mean music, lyrics, and vocals by Nicky Wire, with James Dean Bradfield and Sean Moore providing back-up. This record could also feature an array of guest vocalists to complement and break Wire's crooked croon and even recreate some pop magic moments reminiscent of Wire's vocal contributions to Sarah Cracknel's 2015 single Nothing to Talk About. But mostly I would want a Wire-led record to be a sprawling mix of ragged punk rock and quality pop, a natural spiritual sequel to *Know Your Enemy*. There was talk years ago of a seventy-track triple record (to be titled *70 Songs of Hatred and Failure*) and what better way to fulfil this promise than a collection of short and sharp Wire songs.

An Instrumental Record

The most definitive element of a Manic Street Preacher song is its lyrics. The band has made songs that deal in yearning poetic melancholy for their bread and butter. But glued to these lyrics is music that when at its best glides, bursts, and shimmers, evoking an intensity that rarely sees the light of day in mainstream rock. All three band members are expert musicians who have, over years of playing together, become a symbiotic unit, which sounds cliché, yet is no less true. The band has been playing in the instrumental format for years. The first being Horses Under Starlight, a Bacharach-esq jive that sat as an oddity on the Kevin Carter CD single released in 1996. Since then there have been other examples that usually sit as flipsides on singles releases. You Know It's Going to Hurt, The Vorticists, Ostpolitik, See It

Like Sutherland, Alien Orders/Invisible Armies are prime examples. Only very recently did instrumentals begin cropping up on the main records. Mayakovsky, and Dreaming a City (Hughesovka) were included on the record *Futurology*, evoking the motion through sunlight European cities, passing high-rise blocks and brutalist architecture.

Another pointer to this instrumental adventure would be James Dean Bradfield's hypnotic soundtrack for the 2016 horror film *The Chamber*, which shows a brilliant understanding of communicating a sonic mood without the necessity of lyrics. They could pull off a studio instrumental record with little effort but touring the thing would be out of the question.

The fans demand the right to shout the band's lyrics back, so an instrumental record would have to come during a quiet period, or one of those junctures of reaction when the band intentionally veer into an alternative reality to escape their own past.

Another B-side and Rarities Collection

2002's Lipstick Traces: A Secret History of Manic Street Preachers was a satisfying collection of the band's B-sides, covers, and oddities. The most startling of which was the unheard acoustic stomp of Nirvana's Been a Son. But to any fan of the band, most of these tracks had been heard in their original incarnation as B-sides or live tracks. Since the release of this compilation, the band has racked up a hugely impressive back catalogue of B-sides that have broadened their sound in many ways. One need only look to the B-sides featured on the single releases from *Send Away the Tigers* to understand that a whole other record of anthems was stored in the band's collective brain. The B-sides Anorexic Rodin, Love Letter to The Future, Heyday of The Blood, Boxes and Lists, 1404, and Little Girl Lost would have fit comfortably on the mother record. That these tracks are lost to B-sides is a great shame. So, another archive pummelling collection would be most welcome.

Not long after the release of the single, It's Not War Just the End of Love I made a personal decision to stop buying physical format releases for Manics singles. I have got a few reasons for this, being on the brink of fatherhood was one of them, and knowing disposable income would now be allocated to disposable diapers.

So, apart from excavating YouTube for these tracks, I have no idea of what the band has been releasing as B-sides for almost a decade. This is a big gap in my experience that would be instantly filled by the release of a juicy compilation record.

There is a danger that suggesting these directions at all will inevitably mean they will never be taken. Maybe this is not such a bad thing. The band is currently on a run of hugely successful records and a creative drive most bands in this stage of their careers would have said goodbye to years ago. Veering off into records that offer a challenge to the listener's patience is perhaps unwise in an era where bands can be broken by one underperforming release.

What I have suggested here is what I would consider a fool's errand that would please maybe a minuscule sect of fans.

Whatever the band decides to do in the near future, or by the time of this short book's release, Manic Street Preachers will have mine and many others' attention. They are and remain a formidable band.

THE END

ABOUT THE AUTHOR

Stephen Lee Naish writes about film, politics, and popular culture. He is the author of several books, notably *Create or Die: Essays on the Artistry of Dennis Hopper* and *Riffs and Meaning: Manic Street Preachers and Know Your Enemy*. His work has appeared all over the internet. He lives in Ontario.

For more information about the Modern Music Masters series:
modernmusicmastersuk@gmail.com

Sources

'Manic Street Preachers - Early Demos 1985 - 1990, *Beehive Candy*, August 25, 2011, accessed: 15 - October - 2020. https://www.beehivecandy.com/2011/08/manic-street-preachers-early-demos-1985.html

Price, Simon, Manic Street Preachers Interview: A Heavenly Body of Work - Part One, *The Quietus*, 14 - September - 2008, accessed 03 - October - 2020. https://thequietus.com/articles/00417-manic-street-preachers-a-heavenly-body-of-work

Ibid

Barleby, Bernart, 'Spectators of Suicide', *Antiwar Songs*, 26 - November - 2015, accessed 12 - October - 2020. https://www.antiwarsongs.org/canzone.php?lang=en&id=51005

Price, Simon, Manic Street Preachers Interview: A Heavenly Body of Work - Part One, *The Quietus*, 14 - September - 2008, accessed 03 - October - 2020. https://thequietus.com/articles/00417-manic-street-preachers-a-heavenly-body-of-work

Manic Street Preachers, *Spotify*, Accessed 30 - October - 2020. https://open.spotify.com/artist/2uH0RyPcX7fnCcT90HFDQX

Ginsberg, Allen, 'Howl', *Poetry Foundation,* 1955, Unknown date of publication, accessed 22 - October - 2020. https://www.poetryfoundation.org/poems/49303/howl

Lindsey, Cam, 'Rank Your Records: James Dean Bradfield Rates Manic Street Preachers' 12 Albums' *Vice,* Unknown date or publication, accessed 12 - October - 2020

Johnson, Howard, 'Manic Milton Keynes', Raw, 15 - September - 1993, Accessed 23 - October - 2020. http://www.foreverdelayed.org.uk/msppedia/index.php?title=Manic_Milton_Keynes!_-_RAW,_15th_September_1993

Wright, Lisa, 40 'Essential Manic Street Preachers Tracks', *NME*, 6 - March - 2015, Accessed 13 - October - 2020. https://www.nme.com/list/40-essential-manic-street-preachers-tracks-1339

'Manic Street Preachers - Faster (1994)' *BBC Wales*, 21 May 2009, Accessed 12 - November - 2020. https://www.bbc.co.uk/wales/music/sites/manic-street-preachers/pages/faster_totp.shtml

Wilding, Philip, 'The Manic Street Preachers: Their best songs in their own words', *Louder Sound*, December 12, 2017, Accessed 18 - November - 2020. https://www.loudersound.com/features/the-manic-street-preachers-their-best-songs-in-their-own-words

Renshaw, David, 'Nicky Wire: 'Richey Manic would have the biggest Twitter following in the western world', *NME*, 26 - October - 2012, Accessed 13 - November - 2020.
https://www.nme.com/news/music/manic-street-preachers-82-1248980

Keay, Douglas, Interview for *Woman's Own* ("no such thing as society"), *Woman's Own*, 23 - September - 1987, Accessed 15 - November - 2020.
https://www.margaretthatcher.org/document/106689

Loughrey, Clarisse, 'Noel Gallagher would reform Oasis to stop 'lunatic' Jeremy Corbyn from being Prime Minister', *The Independent*, 06 October 2018, Accessed 11 - November - 2020.
https://www.independent.co.uk/arts-entertainment/music/news/noel-gallagher-oasis-reunion-liam-stop-jeremy-corbyn-labour-wonderwall-a8571676.html

Komlik, Oleg, 'Thatcherism's greatest achievement', *Economic Sociology & Political Economy*, March 19, 2018, Accessed 12 - November - 2020.
https://economicsociology.org/2018/03/19/thatcherisms-greatest-achievement/

Owens, David, 'The story of Manic Millennium, 20 years on from the greatest New Year's Eve party Wales ever saw', *Wales Online*, 31 - December - 2019, accessed 28 - October - 2020.
https://www.walesonline.co.uk/lifestyle/nostalgia/story-manic-millennium-20-years-17492986

Hedges, Chris, 'Death of the Liberal Class (Speech)', Oct 18, 2010, Accessed 12 - December - 2020.
https://www.youtube.com/watch?v=bYCvSntOI5s

Ibid

Williams, Andrew, 'Manic Street Preachers' Nicky Wire on the secret to the band's 30-year success', *Metro*, 20 - April - 2018, accessed 13 - November - 2020.
https://www.metro.news/manic-street-preachers-nicky-wire-on-the-secret-to-the-bands-30-year-success/1024247/

W, Daniel, 'Manic Street Preachers – Send Away the Tigers: 10 Year Collectors' Edition (Album Review)', *Vulture Hound*, 12 - May - 2017, Accessed 19 - November - 2020.
https://vulturehound.co.uk/2017/05/manic-street-preachers-send-away-the-tigers-10-year-collectors-edition-album-review/

Burrows, Mark, Send Away the Tigers (10 Year Collectors' Edition), *Drowned in Sound*, 12 - May - 2017, accessed 14 - November - 2020.
https://drownedinsound.com/releases/19934/reviews/4151025

Nissim, Mayer, 'Ex-GN'R bassist features on new Manics LP', *Digital Spy*, 07 - June - 20, accessed 16 - November - 2020. https://www.digitalspy.com/music/a223960/ex-gnr-bassist-features-on-new-manics-lp/

Ibid

Martin, Dan, 'Manic Street Preachers, 'Postcards from A Young Man' – First Listen', *NME*, 27 - July - 2010, Accessed 17 - November - 2020. https://web.archive.org/web/20121020094742/http://www.nme.com/blog/index.php?blog=140&p=8799&more=1&c=1

Lukowski, Andrzej, 'Manic Street Preachers Postcards from a Young Man', *Drowned in Sound*, 20 - September - 2010, accessed 12 - November - 2020. https://drownedinsound.com/releases/15682/reviews/4141092

Uncut, 'Manic Street Preachers 'gutted' about failing to make the Top 40', *Uncut*, 4 - February - 2011, Accessed 11 - November - 2020. https://www.uncut.co.uk/news/manic-street-preachers-gutted-about-failing-to-make-the-top-40-44006/

Albumism Staff, 'READERS' POLL RESULTS: Your Favorite Manic Street Preachers Album of All Time Revealed', *Albumism*, 23 - October - 2018, accessed 17 - November - 2020. https://www.albumism.com/polls/what-is-your-favorite-manic-street-preachers-album

Maconie, Stuart, 'POSTCARDS FROM A YOUNG MAN', *Journal*, 22 - January - 2014, Accessed 11 - November - 2020. https://www.manicstreetpreachers.com/journal/postcards-young-man/

Owens, David, 'Manic Street Preachers reveal details of new album Rewind the Film and a UK tour', *Wales Online*, 8 - July - 2013, Accessed 12 - November - 2020. https://www.walesonline.co.uk/whats-on/music/manic-street-preachers-reveal-details-4881786

Evans, Kieran, 'ANTHEM FOR A LOST CAUSE' – THE SECOND SINGLE TAKEN FROM THE ALBUM 'REWIND THE FILM', *Manic Street Preachers - News*, 10 - October - 2013, Accessed 16 - November - 2020. https://www.manicstreetpreachers.com/cat-news/anthem-lost-cause-second-single-taken-album-rewind-film/

Trendall, Andrew, 'Manic Street Preachers unveil new video, announce Futurology details', *Gigwise*, 28 - April - 2014, Accessed 13 - November - 2020. https://www.gigwise.com/news/90527/Manic-Street-

Preachers-unveil-new-video-announce-Futurology-details#RYoY7GJJqzjo4KpP.99

 Barker, Emily, NME's Top 50 Tracks of 2014, *NME*, 24 - November - 2014, Accessed 09 - November - 2020. https://www.nme.com/photos/nme-s-top-50-tracks-of-2014-1405699

Trendall, Andrew, 'Manics' Nicky Wire is working on "modern, electronic, soothsaying" solo material', *NME*, 17 - August - 2020, Accessed 03 - December - 2020. https://www.nme.com/news/music/manics-nicky-wire-is-working-on-modern-electronic-soothsaying-solo-material-2730199